Philip Schaff

Saint Chrysostom and Saint Augustin

Philip Schaff

Saint Chrysostom and Saint Augustin

ISBN/EAN: 9783337336417

Printed in Europe, USA, Canada, Australia, Japan

Cover: Foto ©Lupo / pixelio.de

More available books at **www.hansebooks.com**

STUDIES IN CHRISTIAN BIOGRAPHY.

SAINT CHRYSOSTOM

AND

SAINT AUGUSTIN.

BY

PHILIP SCHAFF, D.D., LL.D.,

Professor of Church History in the Union Theological Seminary, New York.

NEW YORK:
THOMAS WHITTAKER,
2 AND 3 BIBLE HOUSE.

Copyright, 1891,
By THOMAS WHITTAKER.

Dedicated

TO THE REVERED MEMORY OF

J. B. LIGHTFOOT, D.D., D.C.L., LL.D.,

Late Lord Bishop of Durham.

PREFACE.

My friend, Mr. Thomas Whittaker, proposes to publish a series of *Studies in Christian Biography*, devoted to the leaders of Christian thought and Christian life, in ancient, mediæval, and modern times.

He requested me to open the series with biographical sketches of St. Chrysostom, the greatest of the Greek, and St. Augustin, the greatest of the Latin Fathers.

To this proposal I readily consented, with the understanding that I could make free use of material which I had previously prepared and recently enlarged as editor of translations of the chief works of these Fathers.*

The memory of St. Chrysostom and St. Augustin can never die. They left their mark on every page of Church history, and their teaching and example will continue to prepare preachers and divines for their work. Petrarch carried the *Confessions* of St. Augustin always in his pocket; he called him "the philosopher of Christ" and "the sun of the Church," and made him his confessor in the autobiographical Dialogue on the *Contempt of the World*. A high admiration of these truly great and good men is quite consistent with an acknowledgment of their defects and errors. There is a safe medium be-

---

* *The Nicene and Post-Nicene Library*, First Series, contains the works of St. Augustin in 8 vols., and the works of St. Chrysostom in 6 vols., with Prolegomena and notes. They were published (as subscription books) by the Christian Literature Company, New York, 1886–90.

tween a slavish overestimate and a haughty underestimate of the Fathers. No man is perfect save Christ, and no man can be our master in the highest sense but Christ. *Amicus Chrysostomus, amicus Augustinus, sed magis amica veritas.*

It was in this spirit of free evangelical catholicity that the lamented Bishop Lightfoot, the greatest patristic scholar of England, prepared his monumental work on the Apostolic Fathers. I have taken the liberty to dedicate this unpretending little volume to his memory. I regret I have nothing more worthy to offer, but I know he would receive it with the kindness of a friend and co-worker in the service of truth. He wrote to me once that he had received the first impulse to his historical studies from my *History of the Apostolic Church;* and yet I have learned more from him than he could ever learn from me. He and Dr. Westcott invited me to contribute to Smith and Wace's *Dictionary of Christian Biography* (then under his charge). He sent me all his works as they appeared. Only a few days ago I received, " with the compliments of the Trustees of the LIGHTFOOT FUND," his posthumous edition of *St. Clement of Rome*, with an autotype of the Constantinopolitan text—a worthy companion of his *St. Ignatius* and *St. Polycarp.* The Bible Revision labors brought us into still closer relations. His book on Revision (which I republished with his consent), and his admirable commentaries on Galatians, Colossians, and Philippians, greatly aided the movement in this country. I shall not forget my pleasant interviews with him at Cambridge, London, Durham, and Auckland Castle. He left a rare example of reverent and modest Christian scholarship that aims first and last at the investigation and promotion of truth.

NEW YORK, December 12, 1890.   P. S.

CONTENTS.

SAINT CHRYSOSTOM.

	PAGE
INTRODUCTORY	11
CHAPTER I. Chrysostom's Youth and Training, A.D. 347–370	13
CHAPTER II. His Conversion and Ascetic Life, A.D. 370–374	15
CHAPTER III. Chrysostom evades Election to a Bishopric. His Work on the Priesthood	18
CHAPTER IV. Chrysostom as a Monk, A.D. 374–381	21
CHAPTER V. Chrysostom as Deacon, Priest and Preacher at Antioch, A.D. 381–398	23
CHAPTER VI. Chrysostom as Patriarch of Constantinople, A.D. 398–404	28
CHAPTER VII. Chrysostom and Theophilus. His First Banishment	30
CHAPTER VIII. Chrysostom and Eudoxia. His Second Banishment, A.D. 403	33
CHAPTER IX. Chrysostom in Exile, and his Death, A.D. 404–407	35
CHAPTER X. His Character	38
CHAPTER XI. The Writings of Chrysostom	41
CHAPTER XII. His Theology and Exegesis	42
CHAPTER XIII. Chrysostom as a Preacher	50
Literature	54

SAINT AUGUSTIN.

INTRODUCTORY	57
CHAPTER I. Augustin's Youth	63
CHAPTER II. Augustin at Carthage	69
CHAPTER III. Cicero's Hortensius	71
CHAPTER IV. Augustin Among the Manichæans	73
CHAPTER V. The Loss of a Friend	76
CHAPTER VI. Augustin Leaves Manichæism	78
CHAPTER VII. Error Overruled for Truth	80

	PAGE
CHAPTER VIII. Augustin a Skeptic in Rome	82
CHAPTER IX. Augustin at Milan. St. Ambrose	85
CHAPTER X. Augustin a Catechisman in the Catholic Church.	91
CHAPTER XI. Monnica's Arrival	96
CHAPTER XII. Moral Conflicts. Project of Marriage	97
CHAPTER XIII. Mental Conflicts	100
CHAPTER XIV. Influence of Platonism	102
CHAPTER XV. Study of the Scriptures	104
CHAPTER XVI. Augustin's Conversion	106
CHAPTER XVII. Sojourn in the Country	113
CHAPTER XVIII. Augustin's Baptism	118
CHAPTER XIX. Monnica's Last Days and Death	120
CHAPTER XX. Second Visit to Rome, and Return to Africa	127
CHAPTER XXI. Augustin is Appointed Priest and Bishop of Hippo	129
CHAPTER XXII. Augustin's Domestic Life	131
CHAPTER XXIII. Administration of the Episcopal Office and Public Activity	133
CHAPTER XXIV. Last Years and Death	136
CHAPTER XXV. Augustin's Writings	138
CHAPTER XXVI. Influence of Augustin on His Own and Succeeding Ages	148
CHAPTER XXVII. The Augustinian System	155
Literature	158

SAINT CHRYSOSTOM.

SAINT CHRYSOSTOM.

"Glory be to God for all things."—Chrysostom's Motto.

INTRODUCTORY.

"Almighty God, who hast given us grace at this time with one accord to make our common supplications unto Thee; and dost promise, that when two or three are gathered together in Thy name Thou wilt grant their requests: fulfil now, O Lord, the desires and petitions of Thy servants, as may be most expedient for them; granting us in this world knowledge of Thy truth, and in the world to come life everlasting. Amen."

THIS beautiful and comprehensive prayer, which is translated from the Greek Liturgy of St. Chrysostom, and goes under his name, has made him a household word wherever the Anglican Book of Common Prayer is known and used.

JOHN, surnamed CHRYSOSTOM (Ἰωάννης Χρυσόστομος), is the greatest pulpit orator and commentator of the Greek Church, and still deservedly enjoys the highest honor in the whole Christian world. No one of the Oriental Fathers has left a more spotless reputation; no one is so much read and so often quoted by modern preachers and commentators. An admiring posterity, since the close of the fifth century, has given him the surname *Chrysostom* (*The Golden Mouth*), which has entirely superseded his personal name *John*, and which best expresses the general estimate of his merits.

His life may be divided into five periods : (1) His youth and training till his conversion and baptism, A.D. 347-70. (2) His conversion, and ascetic and monastic life, 370-81. (3) His public life as priest and preacher at Antioch, 381-98. (4) His episcopate at Constantinople, 398-404. (5) His exile to his death, 404-407.

CHAPTER I.

CHRYSOSTOM'S YOUTH AND TRAINING, A.D. 347–370.

JOHN (the name by which alone he is known among contemporary writers and his first biographers) was born in 347, at Antioch, the capital of Syria, and the home of the mother church of Gentile Christianity, where the disciples of Jesus were first called "Christians."

His father, Secundus, was a distinguished military officer (*magister militum*) in the imperial army of Syria, and died during the infancy of John, without professing Christianity, as far as we know. His mother, Anthusa, was a rare woman. Left a widow at the age of twenty, she refused all offers of marriage, and devoted herself exclusively to the education of her only son and his older sister. She was probably from principle averse to a second marriage, according to a prevailing view of the Fathers. She shines, with Nonna and Monnica, among the most pious mothers of the fourth century, who prove the ennobling influence of Christianity on the character of woman, and through her on all the family relations. Anthusa gained general esteem by her exemplary life. The famous advocate of heathenism, Libanius, on hearing of her consistency and devotion, felt constrained to exclaim: "Bless me! what wonderful women there are among the Christians."

She gave her son the best education then attainable, and early planted in his soul the germs of piety, which afterward bore rich fruits for himself and the Church. By her admonitions and the teaching of the Bible, he was secured against the seductions of heathenism which at that time still was the religion of half of the population of Antioch.

Yet he was not baptized till he had reached the age of maturity. In that period of transition from heathenism to Christianity, the number of adult baptisms far exceeded that of infant baptisms. Hence the large baptisteries, for the baptism of crowds of converts; hence the many sermons and lectures of Chrysostom, Cyril of Jerusalem, and other preachers to catechumens, and their careful instruction before baptism and admission to the Missa Fidelium or the holy communion. Even Christian parents, as the father and mother of Gregory Nazianzen, the mother of Chrysostom, and the mother of Augustin, put off the baptism of their offspring, partly no doubt from a very high conception of baptism as the sacrament of regeneration, and from the superstitious fear that early baptism involved the risk of a forfeiture of baptismal grace. This was the argument which Tertullian in the second century urged against infant baptism, and this was the reason why many professing Christians put off their baptism till the latest hour; just as now so many from the same motive delay repentance and conversion to their death-bed. The Emperor Constantine who favored Christianity as early as 312, and convened the Œcumenical Council of Nicæa in 325, postponed baptism till 337, shortly before his death. The orthodox Emperor Theodosius the Great was not baptized till the first year of his reign (380), when attacked by a serious illness. Chrysostom, however, did not approve such delay, but often rebuked it.

Chrysostom received his literary training chiefly from Libanius, the admirer and friend of the Emperor Julian the Apostate, and the first classical scholar and rhetorician of his age, who after a long career as public teacher at Athens and Constantinople, returned to his native Antioch and had the misfortune to outlive the revival of heathenism under Julian and to lament the triumph of Christianity under his successors. He was introduced by him into a knowledge of the Greek classics and the arts of rhetoric, which served him a good purpose for his future labors in the Church. He was his best scholar, and when Libanius, shortly before his death (about 393), was asked whom he wished for his successor, he replied: "John, if only the Christians had not stolen him from us."

After the completion of his studies Chrysostom became a rhetorician, and began the profitable practice of law, which opened to him a brilliant political career. The amount of litigation was enormous. The display of talent in the law courts was the high-road to the dignities of vice-prefect, prefect, and consul. Some of his speeches at the bar excited admiration and were highly commended by Libanius. For some time, as he says, he was "a never-failing attendant at the courts of law, and passionately fond of the theatre." But he was not satisfied. The temptations of a secular profession in a corrupt state of society discouraged him. To accept a fee for making the worse cause appear the better cause, seemed to him to take Satan's wages.

CHAPTER II.

HIS CONVERSION AND ASCETIC LIFE.

THE quiet study of the Scriptures, the example of his pious mother, the acquaintance with Bishop Meletius, and the influence of his intimate friend Basil, who was of the same age and devoted to ascetic life, combined to produce a gradual change in his character.

He entered the class of catechumens, and after the usual period of three years of instruction and probation, he was baptized by Meletius in his twenty-third year (369 or 370). From this time on, says Palladius, "he neither swore, nor defamed any one, nor spoke falsely, nor cursed, nor even tolerated facetious jokes." His baptism marked, as in the case of St. Augustin, the turning point in his life, an entire renunciation of this world and dedication to the service of Christ. The change was radical and permanent.

Meletius, who foresaw the future greatness of the young lawyer, wished to secure him for the active service of the Church, and ordained him to the subordinate office of lector (anagnostes, reader), about A.D. 370. The lectors had to read the Scripture lessons in the first part of divine service (the "Missa Catechumenorum"), and to call upon the people to pray, but could not preach nor distribute the sacraments.

The first inclination of Chrysostom after baptism was to adopt the monastic life. This was, according to the prevailing notions of the Church in that age, the safest mode of escaping the temptations and corruptions of the world, cultivating holiness, and securing the salvation of the soul. But the earnest entreaties of his mother prevailed on him to delay the gratification of his desire. He relates the scene with dramatic power. She took him to her chamber, and by the bed where she had given him birth, she adjured him with tears not to forsake her. "My son," she said in substance, "my only comfort in the midst of the miseries of this earthly life is to see thee constantly, and to behold in thy traits the faithful image of my beloved husband who is no more. This comfort commenced with your infancy before you could speak. I ask only one favor from you: do not make me a widow a second time; wait at least till I die; perhaps I shall soon leave this world. When you have buried me and joined my ashes with those of your father, nothing will then prevent you from retiring into monastic life. But as long as I breathe, support me by your presence, and do not draw down upon you the wrath of God by bringing such evils upon me who have given you no offence."

These tender, simple, and impressive words suggest many heart-rending scenes caused by the ascetic enthusiasm for separation from the sacred ties of the family. It is honorable to Chrysostom that he yielded to the reasonable wishes of his devoted mother. He remained with her, but turned his home into a monastery. He secluded himself from the world and practised a rigid asceticism. He ate little and seldom, and only the plainest food, slept on the bare floor, and frequently rose to prayer. He kept almost unbroken silence to prevent a relapse into the habit of slander or uncharitable censure.

His former associates at the bar called him unsociable and morose. But two of his fellow-pupils under Libanius joined him in his ascetic life, Maximus (afterward bishop of Seleucia), and Theodore of Mopsuestia. They studied the Scriptures under the direction of Diodorus (afterward bishop of Tarsus), the founder of the Antiochian school of theology, of which Chrysostom and Theodore became the chief ornaments.

Theodore was warmly attached to a young lady named Hermione, and resolved to marry and to leave the ascetic brotherhood. This gave rise to the earliest treatise of Chrysostom—namely, an Exhortation to Theodore, in two letters. He plied all his oratorical arts of sad sympathy, tender entreaty, bitter reproach, and terrible warning, to reclaim his friend to what he thought the surest and safest way to heaven. "To sin," he says, "is human, but to persist in sin is devilish; to fall is not ruinous to the soul, but to remain on the ground is."

The appeal had its desired effect; Theodore resumed his monastic life and became afterward bishop of Mopsuestia in Cilicia and one of the first biblical scholars. The arguments which Chrysostom used would condemn all who broke their monastic vows. They retain moral force only if we substitute apostasy from faith for apostasy from monasticism, which must be regarded as a temporary and abnormal or exceptional form of Christian life.

CHAPTER III.

CHRYSOSTOM EVADES ELECTION TO A BISHOPRIC. HIS WORK ON THE PRIESTHOOD.

ABOUT this time several bishoprics were vacant in Syria, and frequent depositions took place with the changing fortunes of orthodoxy and Arianism, and the interference of the court. The attention of the clergy and the people turned to Chrysostom and his friend Basil as suitable candidates for the episcopal office, although they had not the canonical age of thirty.

Chrysostom shrunk from the responsibilities and avoided an election by a pious fraud. He apparently assented to an agreement with Basil that both should either accept, or resist the burden of the episcopate, but instead of that he concealed himself and put forward his friend whom he accounted much more worthy of the honor. Basil, under the impression that Chrysostom had already been consecrated, reluctantly submitted to the election. When he discovered the cheat, he upbraided his friend with the breach of compact, but Chrysostom laughed and rejoiced at the success of his plot. This conduct, which every sound Christian conscience must condemn, caused no offence among the Christians of that age, still less among the heathen, and was regarded as good management or "economy." The moral character of the deception was supposed to depend altogether on the motive, which made it good or bad. Chrysostom appealed in justification of laudable deception to the stratagems of war, to the conduct of physicians in dealing with refractory patients, to several examples of the Old Testament (Abraham, Jacob, David), and to the conduct of the Apostle Paul in circumcising Timothy for the sake of the Jews (Acts xvi. 3) and in observing the ceremonial law in Jerusalem at the advice of James (Acts xxi. 26).

The Jesuitical maxim, "the end justifies the means," is much older than Jesuitism, and runs through the whole apocryphal, pseudo-prophetic, pseudo-apostolic, pseudo-Clementine and pseudo-Isidorian literature of the early centuries. Several of the best Fathers show a surprising want of a strict sense of veracity. They introduce a sort of cheat even into their strange theory of redemption, by supposing that the Devil caused the crucifixion under the delusion that Christ was a mere man, and thus lost his claim upon the fallen race. Origen, Chrysostom, and Jerome explain the offence of the collision between Paul and Peter at Antioch (Gal. ii. 11 sqq.) away by turning it into a theatrical and hypocritical farce, which was shrewdly arranged by the two apostles for the purpose of convincing the Jewish Christians that circumcision was not necessary. Against such wretched exegesis the superior moral sense of Augustin rightly protested, and Jerome changed his view on this particular passage. Here is a point where the modern standard of ethics is far superior to that of the Fathers, and more fully accords with the spirit of the New Testament, which inculcates the strictest veracity as a fundamental virtue.

The escape from the episcopate was the occasion for one of the best and most popular works of Chrysostom, the six books "On the Priesthood," which he wrote probably before his ordination (between 375 and 381), or during his diaconate (between 381 and 386). It is composed in the form of a Platonic dialogue between Chrysostom and Basil. He first vindicates by argument and examples his well-meant but untruthful conduct toward his friend, and the advantages of timely fraud; and then describes with youthful fervor and eloquence the importance, duties, and trials of the Christian ministry, without distinguishing between the priestly and the episcopal office. He elevates it above all other offices. He requires whole-souled consecration to Christ and love to his flock. He points to the Scriptures (quoting also from the Apocrypha) as the great weapon of the minister. He assumes, as may be expected, the then prevailing conception of a real priesthood and sacrifice, baptismal regeneration, the corporal presence, the virtue of absolution, prayers for the dead, but is silent about pope and councils, the orders of the clergy, prayers to saints, forms of prayer, priestly vestments, incense, crosses and other doctrines and ceremonies of the Greek and Roman churches. He holds up St. Paul as a model for imitation. The sole object of the preacher must be to please God rather than men (Gal. i. 10). "He must not indeed despise approving demonstrations, but as little must he court them, nor trouble himself when they are withheld." He should combine the qualities of dignity and humility, authority and sociability, impartiality and courtesy, independence and lowliness, strength and gentleness, and keep a single eye to the glory of Christ and the welfare of the Church.

This book is the most useful or at least the best known among the works of Chrysostom, and is well calculated to inspire a profound sense of the tremendous responsibilities of the ministry. But it has serious defects, besides the objectionable justification of pious fraud, and cannot satisfy the demands of an evangelical minister. In all that pertains to the proper care of souls it is inferior to the "Reformed Pastor" of Richard Baxter.

CHAPTER IV.

CHRYSOSTOM AS A MONK. A.D. 374–381.

AFTER the death of his mother, Chrysostom fled from the seductions and tumults of city life to the monastic solitude of the mountains south of Antioch, and there spent six happy years in theological study and sacred meditation and prayer. Monasticism was to him (as to many other great teachers of the Church, and even to Luther) a profitable school of spiritual experience and self-government. He embraced this mode of life as "the true philosophy" from the purest motives, and brought into it intellect and cultivation enough to make the seclusion available for moral and spiritual growth.

He gives us a lively description of the bright side of this monastic life. The monks lived in separate cells or huts (καλύβαι), but according to a common rule and under the authority of an abbot. They wore coarse garments of camel's hair or goat's hair over their linen tunics. They rose before sunrise, and began the day by singing a hymn of praise and common prayer under the leadership of the abbot. Then they went to their allotted task, some to read, others to write, others to manual labor for the support of the poor. Four hours in each day were devoted to prayer and singing. Their only food was bread and water, except in case of sickness. They slept on straw couches, free from care and anxiety. There was no need of bolts and bars. They held all things in common, and the words of "mine and thine," which cause innumerable strifes in the world, were unknown among the brethren. If one died, he caused no lamentation, but thanksgiving, and was carried to the grave amid hymns of praise; for he was not dead, but "perfected," and permitted to behold the face of Christ. For them to live was Christ, and to die was gain.

Chrysostom was an admirer of active and useful monasticism, and warns against the dangers of idle contemplation. He shows that the words of our Lord, "One thing is needful;" "Take no anxious thought for the morrow;" "Labor not for the meat that perisheth," do not inculcate total abstinence from work, but only undue anxiety about worldly things, and must be harmonized with the apostolic exhortation to labor and to do good. He defends monastic seclusion on account of the prevailing immorality in the cities, which made it almost impossible to cultivate there a higher Christian life.

In this period, from 374 to 381, Chrysostom composed his earliest writings in praise of monasticism and celibacy.

The letters "to the fallen Theodore," have already been mentioned. The three books against the Opponents of Monasticism were occasioned by a decree of the Arian Emperor Valens in 373, which aimed at the destruction of that system and compelled the monks to discharge their duties to the state by military or civil service. Chrysostom regarded this decree as a sacrilege, and the worst kind of persecution.

CHAPTER V.

CHRYSOSTOM AS DEACON, PRIEST, AND PREACHER AT ANTIOCH. A.D. 381–398.

By excessive self-mortifications John undermined his health, and returned to Antioch. There he was immediately ordained deacon by Meletius in 380 or 381, and a few years afterward presbyter by Flavian (386).

As deacon he had the best opportunity to become acquainted with the practical needs of the population, the care of the poor and the sick. After his ordination to the priesthood he preached in the presence of the bishop his first sermon to a vast crowd. It abounds in flowery Asiatic eloquence, in humble confession of his own unworthiness, and exaggerated praise of Meletius and Flavian.

He now entered upon a large field of usefulness, the real work of his life. The pulpit was his throne, and he adorned it as much as any preacher of ancient or modern times.

Antioch was one of the great capitals of the Roman empire, along with Alexandria, Constantinople, and

Rome. Nature and art combined to make it a delightful residence, though it was often visited by inundations and earthquakes. An abundance of pure water from the river Orontes, a large lake and the surrounding hills, fertile plains, the commerce of the sea, imposing buildings of Asiatic, Greek, and Roman architecture, rich gardens, baths, and colonnaded streets, were among its chief attractions. A broad street of four miles, built by Antiochus Epiphanes, traversed the city from east to west; the spacious colonnades on either side were paved with red granite. Innumerable lanterns illuminated the main thoroughfares at night. The city was supplied with good schools and several churches; the greatest of them, in which Chrysostom preached, was begun by the Emperor Constantine and finished by Constantius. The inhabitants were Syrians, Greeks, Jews, and Romans. The Asiatic element prevailed. The whole population amounted, as Chrysostom states, to 200,000, of whom one-half were nominally Christians. Heathenism was therefore still powerful as to numbers, but as a religion it had lost all vitality. This was shown by the failure of the attempt of the Emperor Julian the Apostate to revive the sacrifices to the gods. When he endeavored, in 362, to restore the oracle of Apollo Daphneus in the famous cypress grove at Antioch and arranged for a magnificent procession, with libation, dances, and incense, he found in the temple one solitary old priest, and this priest ominously offered in sacrifice—a goose! Julian himself relates this ludicrous farce, and vents his anger at the Antiochians for squandering the rich incomes of the temple upon Christianity, and worldly amusements.

Chrysostom gives us in his sermons lively pictures of the character of the people and the condition of the Church. The prevailing vices, even among Christians, were avarice, luxury, sensuality, and excessive love of the circus and the theatre. "So great," he says, "is the depravity of the times, that if a stranger were to compare the precepts of the gospel with the actual practice of society, he would infer that men were not the disciples, but the enemies of Christ." Gibbon thus describes the morals of Antioch: "The warmth of the climate disposed the natives to the most intemperate enjoyment of tranquillity and opulence, and the lively licentiousness of the Greeks was blended with the hereditary softness of the Syrians. Fashion was the only law, pleasure the only pursuit, and the splendor of dress and furniture was the only distinction of the citizens of Antioch. The arts of luxury were honored, the serious and manly virtues were the subject of ridicule, and the contempt for female modesty and reverent age announced the universal corruption of the capital of the East. The love of spectacles was the taste, or rather passion of the Syrians; the most skilful artists were procured from the adjacent cities. A considerable share of the revenue was devoted to the public amusements, and the magnificence of the games of the theatre and circus was considered as the happiness and as the glory of Antioch."

The Church of Antioch was rent for eighty-five years (330–415) by heresy and schism. There were three parties and as many rival bishops. The Meletians, under the lead of Meletius, were the party of moderate orthodoxy holding the Nicene Creed; the Arians, headed by Eudoxius, and supported by the Emperor Valens, denied the eternal divinity of Christ; the Eustathians, under the venerated priest Paulinus, were in communion with Athanasius, but were accused of Sabellianism, which maintained the Divine unity and strict deity of Christ and the Holy Spirit, but denied the tri-personality except in the form of three modes of self-revelation. Pope Damasus declared for Paulinus and condemned Meletius as a heretic. Alexandria likewise sided against him. Meletius was more than once banished from his see, and recalled. He died during the sessions of the Council of Constantinople, 381, over which he presided for a while. His remains were carried with great solemnities to Antioch and buried by the side of Babylas the Martyr. Chrysostom reconciled Flavian, the successor of Meletius, with Alexandria and Rome in 398. Alexander, the successor of Flavian, led the Eustathians back into the orthodox Church in 415, and thus unity was restored.

Chrysostom preached Sunday after Sunday, and during Lent sometimes twice or oftener during the week, even five days in succession, on the duties and responsibilities of Christians, and fearlessly attacked the immorality of the city. He declaimed with special severity against the theatre and the chariot-races; and yet many of his hearers would run from his sermons to the circus to witness those exciting spectacles with the same eagerness as Jews and Gentiles. He exemplified his preaching by a blameless life, and soon acquired great reputation and won the love of the whole congregation. Whenever he preached the church was crowded. He had to warn his hearers against pickpockets, who found an inviting harvest in these dense audiences.

A serious disturbance which took place during his career at Antioch, called forth a remarkable effort of his oratorical powers. The populace of the city, provoked by excessive taxes, rose in revolt against the Emperor Theodosius the Great, broke down his statues and those of his deceased excellent wife Flacilla (d. 385), and his son Arcadius, dragged the fragments through the streets, and committed other acts of violence. The Emperor threatened to destroy the whole city. This caused general consternation and agony, but the city was saved by the intercession of Bishop Flavian, who in his old age proceeded to Constantinople and secured free pardon from the Emperor. Although a man of violent temper, Theodosius had profound reverence for bishops, and on another occasion he submitted to the rebuke of St. Ambrose for the wholesale massacre of the Thessalonians (390).

In this period of public anxiety, which lasted several months, Chrysostom delivered a series of extempore orations, in which he comforted the people and exhorted them to correct their vices. These are his twenty-one "Homilies on the Statues," so-called from the overthrow of the imperial statues which gave rise to them. They were preached during Lent 387. In the same year St. Augustin submitted to baptism at the hands of St. Ambrose in Milan. One of the results of those sermons was the conversion of a large number of heathens. Thus the calamity was turned into a blessing to the Church.

During the sixteen or seventeen years of his labors in Antioch Chrysostom wrote the greater part of his homilies and commentaries; a consolatory epistle to the despondent Stagirius; the excellent book on the martyr Babylas, which illustrates by a striking example the divine power of Christianity; a treatise on Virginity, which he puts above marriage; and an admonition to a young widow on the glory of widowhood, and the duty of continuing in it. He disapproved of second marriage, not as sinful or illegal, but as inconsistent with an ideal conception of marriage and a high order of piety.

CHAPTER VI.

CHRYSOSTOM AS PATRIARCH OF CONSTANTINOPLE. A.D. 398–404.

After the death of Nectarius (successor to Gregory Nazianzen), toward the end of the year 397, Chrysostom was chosen, entirely without his own agency and even against his remonstrance, archbishop of Constantinople. He was hurried away from Antioch by a military escort, to avoid a commotion in the congregation and to make resistance useless. He was consecrated February 26th, 398, by his enemy Theophilus, patriarch of Alexandria, who reluctantly yielded to the command of the Emperor Arcadius or rather his prime minister, the eunuch Eutropius, and nursed his revenge for a more convenient season.

Constantinople, built by Constantine the Great in 330, on the site of Byzantium, assumed as the Eastern capital of the Roman Empire the first position among the episcopal sees of the East, and became the centre of court theology, court intrigues, and theological controversies. The second œcumenical council, which was held there in 381, under Theodosius the Great, the last Roman emperor worthy of the name (d. 395), decided the victory of Nicene orthodoxy over the Arian heresy, and gave the bishop of Constantinople a primacy of honor, next in rank to the bishop of old Rome,—a position which was afterward confirmed by the Council of Chalcedon in 451, but disputed by Pope Leo and his successors.

Chrysostom soon gained by his eloquent sermons the admiration of the people, of the weak Emperor Arcadius, and, at first, even of his wife Eudoxia, with whom he afterward waged a deadly war. He extended his pastoral care to the Goths who were becoming numerous in Constantinople, had a part of the Bible translated for them, often preached to them himself through an interpreter, and sent missionaries to the Gothic and Scythian tribes on the Danube. He continued to direct by correspondence these missionary operations even during his exile. For a short time he enjoyed the height of power and popularity.

But he also made enemies by his denunciations of the vices and follies of the clergy and aristocracy. He emptied the episcopal palace of its costly plate and furniture and sold them for the benefit of the poor and the hospitals. He introduced his strict ascetic habits and reduced the luxurious household of his predecessors to the strictest simplicity. He devoted his large income to benevolence. He refused invitations to banquets, gave no dinner parties, and ate the simplest fare in his solitary chamber. He denounced unsparingly luxurious habits in eating and dressing, and enjoined upon the rich the duty of almsgiving to an extent that tended to increase rather than diminish the number of beggars who swarmed in the streets and around the churches and public baths. He disciplined the vicious clergy and opposed the perilous and immoral habit of unmarried priests of living under the same roof with "spiritual sisters." This habit dated from an earlier age, and was a reaction against celibacy. Cyprian had raised his protest against it, and the Council of Nicæa forbade unmarried priests to live with any females except close relations. Chrysostom's unpopularity was increased by his irritability and obstinacy, and his subservience to a proud and violent archdeacon, Serapion. The Empress Eudoxia was jealons of his influence over her husband, Arcadius, and angry at his uncompromising severity against sin and vice. She became the chief instrument of his downfall.

The occasion was furnished by an unauthorized use of his episcopal power beyond the lines of his diocese, which was confined to the city. At the request of the clergy of Ephesus and the neighboring bishops, he visited that city in January, 401, held a synod and deposed six bishops convicted of shameful simony. During his absence of several months he left the episcopate of Constantinople in the hands of Severian, bishop of Gabala, an unworthy and adroit flatterer, who basely betrayed his trust and formed a cabal headed by the Empress and her licentious court ladies, for the ruin of Chrysostom. On his return he used unguarded language in the pulpit, and spoke of Elijah's relation to Jezebel in a manner that Eudoxia understood it as a personal insult. The clergy were anxious to get rid of a bishop who was too severe for their lax morals.

CHAPTER VII.

CHRYSOSTOM AND THEOPHILUS.   HIS FIRST BANISHMENT

At this time Chrysostom became involved in the Origenistic controversies which are among the most violent and most useless in ancient Church history, and full of personal invective and calumny. The object in dispute was the orthodoxy of the great Origen, which long after his death was violently assailed and as violently defended.

Theophilus of Alexandria, an able and vigorous but

domineering, contentious and unscrupulous prelate, was at first an admirer of Origen, but afterward in consequence of a personal quarrel joined the opponents, condemned his memory and banished the Origenistic monks from Egypt. Some fifty of them, including the four "Tall Brethren," so-called on account of their extraordinary stature, fled to Constantinople and were hospitably received by Chrysostom (401). He had no sympathy with the philosophical speculations of Origen, but appreciated his great merits, and felt that injustice was done to the persecuted monks. He interceded in their behalf with Theophilus, who replied with indignant remonstrance against protecting heretics and interfering with the affairs of another diocese.

Theophilus, long desirous of overthrowing Chrysostom, whom he had reluctantly consecrated, set every instrument in motion to take revenge. He sent the octogenarian bishop Epiphanius of Salamis, a well-meaning and learned but bigoted zealot for orthodoxy, to Constantinople, as a tool of his hierarchical plans (402); but Epiphanius soon returned and died on the ship (403). Theophilus now travelled himself to Constantinople, accompanied by a body-guard of rough sailors and provided with splendid presents. He appeared at once as accuser and judge, aided by Eudoxia and the disaffected clergy. He held a secret council of thirty-six bishops, all of them Egyptians, except seven, in a suburb of Chalcedon on the Asiatic side of the Bosphorus, and procured in this so-called synod at the Oak, the deposition and banishment of Chrysostom, on false charges of immorality and high treason (403). Among the twenty-nine charges were these: that Chrysostom had called the saintly Epiphanius a fool and a demon, that he abused the clergy, that he received females without witnesses, that he ate sumptuously alone and bathed alone, that he had compared the Empress with Jezebel.

The innocent bishop refused to appear before a packed synod of his enemies, and appealed to a general council. As the sentence of banishment for life became known, the indignation of the people was immense. A single word from him would have raised an insurrection; but he surrendered himself freely to the imperial officers, who conveyed him in the dark to the harbor and put him on board a ship destined for Hieron at the mouth of the Pontus. Theophilus entered the city in triumph and took vengeance on Chrysostom's friends.

The people besieged the palace and demanded the restoration of their bishop. Constantinople was almost in a state of insurrection. The following night the city was convulsed by an earthquake, which was felt with peculiar violence in the bedroom of Eudoxia and frightened her into submission. She implored the Emperor to avert the wrath of God by recalling Chrysostom. Messengers were despatched with abject apologies to bring him back. A whole fleet of barks put forth to greet him, the Bosphorus blazed with torches and resounded with songs of rejoicing. On passing the gates he was borne aloft by the people to the church, seated in the episcopal chair and forced to make an address. His triumph was complete, but of short duration. Theophilus felt unsafe in Constantinople and abruptly sailed in the night for Alexandria.

The feelings with which Chrysostom went into his first and second exile, he well describes in a letter to Bishop Cyriacus: "When I was driven from the city, I felt no anxiety, but said to myself: If the Empress wishes to banish me, let her do so; 'the earth is the Lord's.' If she wants to have me sawn asunder, I have

Isaiah for an example. If she wants me to be drowned in the ocean, I think of Jonah. If I am to be thrown into the fire, the three men in the furnace suffered the same. If cast before wild beasts, I remember Daniel in the lion's den. If she wants me to be stoned, I have before me Stephen, the first martyr. If she demands my head, let her do so; John the Baptist shines before me. Naked I came from my mother's womb, naked shall I leave this world. Paul reminds me, 'If I still pleased men, I would not be the servant of Christ.'"

CHAPTER VIII.

CHRYSOSTOM AND EUDOXIA. HIS SECOND BANISHMENT, A.D. 403.

The restored patriarch and the repentant Empress seemed reconciled, and vied with one another in extravagant and hypocritical laudations for two months, when the feud broke out afresh and ended in Chrysostom's perpetual exile and death.

Eudoxia was a beautiful, imperious, intriguing and revengeful woman, who despised her husband and indulged her passions. Not content with the virtual rule of the Roman Empire, she aspired to semi-divine honors, such as used to be paid to the heathen Cæsars. A column of porphyry with her silver statue for public adoration was erected in September, 403, on the forum before the church of St. Sophia, and dedicated amid boisterous and licentious revelry, which disturbed the sacred services.

Chrysostom ascended the pulpit on the commemoration day of the martyrdom of John the Baptist, and thundered his righteous indignation against all who shared in these profane amusements, the people, the prefect, and the haughty woman on the throne. In the heat of his zeal the imprudent words are said to have escaped his lips: "Again Herodias is raging, again she is dancing, again she demands the head of John on a platter." The comparison of Eudoxia with Herodias, and of himself (John) with John the Baptist was offensively personal, like his former allusion to the relation of Jezebel and Elijah. Whether he really spoke these or similar words is at least doubtful, but they were reported to Eudoxia, who as a woman and an empress could never forgive such an insult. She demanded from the Emperor signal redress. In the conflict of imperial and episcopal authority the former achieved a physical and temporary, the latter a moral and enduring victory.

The enemies of Chrysostom flocked like vultures down to their prey. Theophilus directed the plot from a safe distance. Arcadius was persuaded to issue an order for the removal of Chrysostom. He continued to preach and refused to leave the church over which God had placed him, but he had to yield to armed force. He was dragged by imperial guards from the cathedral on the vigil of the resurrection in 404, while the sacrament of baptism was being administered to hundreds of catechumens. "The waters of regeneration," says Palladius, "were stained with blood." The female candidates, half-dressed, were driven by licentious soldiers into the dark streets. The eucharistic elements were profaned by pagan hands. The clergy in their priestly robes were ejected and chased through the city. The horrors of that night were long afterward remembered with a shudder. During the greater part of the Easter week the city was kept in a state of consternation. Private dwellings were invaded, and suspected Joannites—the partisans of Chrysostom—thrown into prison, scourged, and tortured. Chrysostom, who was shut up in his episcopal palace, twice narrowly escaped assassination.

At last on June 5, 404, the timid and long-hesitating Arcadius signed the edict of banishment. Chrysostom received it with calm submission, and after a final prayer in the cathedral with some of his faithful bishops, and a tender farewell to his beloved Olympias and her attendant deaconesses, he surrendered himself to the guards and was conveyed at night to the Asiatic shore. He had scarcely left the city, when the cathedral was consumed by fire. The charge of incendiarism was raised against his friends, but neither threats, nor torture and mutilation could elicit a confession of guilt. He refused to acknowledge Arsacius and Atticus as his successors; and this was made a crime punishable with degradation, fine, and imprisonment. The clergy who continued faithful to him were deposed and banished. Pope Innocent of Rome was appealed to, pronounced the synod which had condemned Chrysostom irregular, annulled the deposition, and wrote him a letter of sympathy. He urged upon Arcadius the convocation of a general council, but without effect.

CHAPTER IX.

CHRYSOSTOM IN EXILE, AND HIS DEATH.   A.D. 404–407.

Chrysostom was conveyed under the scorching heat of July and August over Galatia and Cappadocia, to the lonely mountain village Cucusus, on the borders of

Cilicia and Armenia, which the wrath of Eudoxia had selected for his exile. The climate was inclement and variable, the winter severe, the place was exposed to Isaurian brigands. He suffered much from fever and headache, and was more than once brought to the brink of the grave. Nevertheless the bracing mountain air invigorated his feeble constitution, and he was hopeful of returning to his diocese. He was kindly treated by the bishop of Cucusus. He received visits, letters, and presents from faithful friends, and by his correspondence exerted a wider influence from that solitude than from the episcopal throne.

His 242 extant letters are nearly all from the three years of his exile, and breathe a noble Christian spirit, in a clear, brilliant, and persuasive style. They exhibit his faithful care for all the interests of the Church and look calmly and hopefully to the glories of heaven. They are addressed to Eastern and Western bishops, presbyters, deacons, deaconesses, monks and missionaries; they describe the fatigues of his journey, give advice on a variety of subjects, strengthen and comfort his distant flock, urge the destruction of heathen temples in Phœnicia, the extirpation of heresy in Cyprus, and encourage the missions in Persia and Scythia. Two letters are addressed to the Roman bishop Innocent I., whose sympathy and assistance he courted. Seventeen letters—the most important of all—are addressed to Olympias, the deaconess, a widow of noble birth, personal beauty and high accomplishments, who devoted her fortune and time to the poor and the sick. She died between 408 and 420. To her he revealed his inner life, and upon her virtues he lavished extravagant praise, which offends modern taste as fulsome flattery. For her consolation he wrote a special treatise on the theme that "No one is really injured except by himself."

The cruel Empress, stung by disappointment at the continued power of the banished bishop, forbade all correspondence and ordered his transfer by two brutal guards, first to Arabissus, then to Pityus on the Caucasus, the most inhospitable spots in the empire.

The journey of three months on foot was a slow martyrdom to the feeble and sickly old man. He did not reach his destination, but ended his pilgrimage five or six miles from Comana in Pontus in the chapel of the martyr Basiliscus on September 14th, 407, in his sixtieth year, the tenth of his episcopate. Clothed in his white baptismal robes, he partook of the eucharist and commended his soul to God. His last words were his accustomed doxology, the motto of his life: "Glory be to God for all things, Amen."

He was buried by the side of Basiliscus in the presence of monks and nuns.

He was revered as a saint by the people. Thirty-one years after his death, January 27, 438, his body was translated with great pomp to Constantinople and deposited with the emperors and patriarchs beneath the altar of the church of the Holy Apostles. The young Emperor Theodosius II. and his sister Pulcheria met the procession at Chalcedon, knelt down before the coffin, and in the name of their guilty parents implored the forgiveness of Heaven for the grievous injustice done to the greatest and saintliest man that ever graced the pulpit and episcopal chair of Constantinople. The Eastern Church of that age shrunk from the bold speculations of Origen, but revered the narrow orthodoxy of Epiphanius, and the ascetic piety of Chrysostom.

The personal appearance of the golden-mouthed orator

was not imposing, but dignified and winning. He was of small stature (like David, Paul, Athanasius, Melanchthon, John Wesley, Schleiermacher). He had an emaciated frame, a large, bald head, a lofty, wrinkled forehead, deep-set, bright, piercing eyes, pallid, hollow cheeks, and a short, gray beard.

CHAPTER X.

HIS CHARACTER.

CHRYSOSTOM was one of those rare men who combine greatness and goodness, genius and piety, and continue to exercise by their writings and example a happy influence upon the Christian Church. He was a man for his time and for all times. But we must look at the spirit rather than the form of his piety, which bore the stamp of his age.

He took Paul for his model, but had a good deal of the practical spirit of James, and of the fervor and loveliness of John. The Scriptures were his daily food, and he again and again recommended their study to laymen as well as ministers. He was not an ecclesiastical statesman, like St. Ambrose, not a profound divine like St. Augustin, but a pure man, a practical Christian, and a king of preachers. "He carried out in his own life," says Hase, "as far as mortal man can do it, the ideal of the priesthood which he once described in youthful enthusiasm." He considered it the duty of every Christian to promote the spiritual welfare of his fellowmen. "Nothing can be more chilling," he says in his twentieth homily on Acts, "than the sight of a Christian who makes no effort to save others. Neither poverty, nor humble station, nor bodily infirmity can exempt men and women from the obligation of this great duty. To hide our light under pretense of weakness is as great an insult to God as if we were to say that He could not make His sun to shine."

It is very much to his praise that in an age of narrow orthodoxy and dogmatic intolerance he cherished a catholic and irenical spirit. He by no means disregarded the value of theological soundness, and was in hearty agreement with the Nicene Creed, which triumphed over the Arians during his ministry in Antioch. But he took no share in the persecution of heretics, and even sheltered the Origenistic monks against the violence of Theophilus of Alexandria. He hated sin more than error, and placed charity above orthodoxy.

Like all the Nicene Fathers, he was an enthusiast for ascetic and monastic virtue, which shows itself in seclusion rather than in transformation of the world and the natural ordinances of God. He retained as priest and bishop his cloister habits of simplicity, abstemiousness and unworldliness. He presents the most favorable aspect of that mode of life, which must be regarded as a wholesome reaction against the hopeless corruption of pagan society. He thought with St. Paul that he could best serve the Lord in single life, and no one can deny that he was unreservedly devoted to the cause of religion.

He was not a man of affairs, and knew little of the world. He had the harmlessness of the dove without the wisdom of the serpent. He knew human nature better than individual men. In this respect he resembles Neander, his best German biographer. Besides, he was irritable, suspicious of his enemies, and easily deceived and misled by such men as Scrapion. He showed these defects in his quarrel with the court and the aristocracy of Constantinople. With a little more worldly wisdom and less ascetic severity he might perhaps have conciliated and converted those whom he repelled by his pulpit fulminations. Fearless denunciation of immorality and vice in high places always commands admiration and respect, especially in a bishop and court preacher who is exposed to the temptations of flattery. But it is unwise to introduce personalities into the pulpit and does more harm than good. His relation to Eudoxia reminds one of the attitude of John Knox to Mary Stuart. The contrast between the pure and holy zeal of the preacher and the reformer and the ambition and vanity of a woman on the throne is very striking and must be judged by higher rules than those of gallantry and courtesy. But after all, the conduct of Christ, the purest of the pure, toward Mary Magdalene and the woman taken in adultery is far more sublime. Mercy is better than justice.

The conflict of Chrysostom with Eudoxia imparts to his later life the interest of a romance, and was overruled for his benefit. In his exile his character shines even brighter than in the pulpit of Antioch and Constantinople. His character was perfected by suffering. The gentleness, meekness, patience, endurance and devotion to his friends and to his work which he showed during the last three years of his life, are the crowning glory of his career. Though he did not die a violent death, he deserves to be numbered among the true martyrs, who are ready for any sacrifice to the cause of virtue and piety.

CHAPTER XI.

THE WRITINGS OF CHRYSOSTOM.[*]

CHRYSOSTOM was the most fruitful author among the Greek Fathers. Suidas makes the extravagant remark that only the omniscient God could recount all his writings. The best have been preserved and have already been noticed in chronological order. They may be divided into five classes: (1) Moral and ascetic treatises, including the work on the priesthood; (2) about six hundred homilies and commentaries; (3) occasional, festal and panegyrical orations; (4) letters; (5) liturgy.

His most important and permanently useful works are his homilies and commentaries, which fill eleven of the thirteen folio volumes of the Benedictine edition. They go together; his homilies are expository, and his commentaries are homiletical and practical. Continuous expositions, according to chapter and verse, he wrote only on the first six chapters of Isaiah, and on the Epistle to the Galatians. All others are arranged in sermons with a moral application at the close. Suidas and Cassiodorus state that he wrote commentaries on the whole Bible. We have from him homilies on Genesis, the Psalms, the Gospel of Matthew, the Gospel of John, the Acts, the Pauline Epistles, including the Hebrews, which he considered Pauline. Besides, he delivered discourses on separate texts of Scripture, on Church festivals, eulogies

---

[*] An English translation of his principal works was edited by Schaff in the first series of "A Select Library of the Nicene and Post-Nicene Fathers of the Christian Church," published by the Christian Literature Company, New York, 1889-'90, vols. ix.-xiv.

on apostles and martyrs, sermons against the pagans, against the Jews and Judaizing Christians, against the Arians, and the famous twenty-one orations on the Statues.

He published some of his sermons himself, but most of them were taken down by short-hand writers. Written sermons were the exceptions in those days. The preacher usually was seated, the people were standing.

Of the letters of Chrysostom we have already spoken.

The liturgy of St. Chrysostom so-called is an abridgment and improvement of the liturgy of St. Basil (d. 379), and both are descended from the liturgy of James, which they superseded. They have undergone gradual changes. It is impossible to determine the original text, as no two copies precisely agree. Chrysostom frequently refers to different parts of the divine service customary in his day, but there is no evidence that he composed a full liturgy, nor is it probable. The liturgy which bears his name is still used in the orthodox Greek and Russian Church on all Sundays, except those during Lent, and on the eve of Epiphany, Easter, and Christmas, when the liturgy of Basil takes its place

CHAPTER XII.

HIS THEOLOGY AND EXEGESIS.

CHRYSOSTOM belonged to the Antiochian school of theology and exegesis, and is its soundest and most popular representative. It was founded by his teacher Diodor of Tarsus (d. 393), developed by himself and his fellow-student Theodore of Mopsuestia (d. 429), and followed by Theodoret and the Syrian and Nestorian divines. Theodore was the exegete, Chrysostom the homilist, Theodoret the annotator. The school was afterward condemned for its alleged connection with the Nestorian heresy; but that connection was accidental, not necessary. Chrysostom's mind was not given to dogmatizing, and too well balanced to run into heresy.

The Antiochian school agreed with the Alexandrian school founded by Origen, in maintaining the divine inspiration and authority of the Scriptures, but differed from it in the method of interpretation, and in a sharper distinction between the Old and the New Testaments, and the divine and human elements in the same.

To Origen belongs the great merit of having broken the path of biblical science and criticism, but he gave the widest scope to the allegorizing and mystical method by which the Bible may be made to say anything that is pious and edifying. Philo of Alexandria had used that method for introducing the Platonic philosophy into the Mosaic writings. Origen was likewise a Platonist, but his chief object was to remove all that was offensive in the literal sense. The allegorical method is imposition rather than exposition. Christ sanctions parabolic teaching and typical, but not allegorical, interpretation. Paul uses it once or twice, but only incidentally, when arguing from the rabbinical standpoint.

The Antiochian school seeks to explain the obvious grammatical and historical sense, which is rich enough for all purposes of instruction and edification. It takes out of the Word what is actually in it, instead of putting into it all sorts of foreign notions and fancies.

Chrysostom recognizes allegorizing in theory, but seldom uses it in practice, and then more by way of rhetorical ornament and in deference to custom. He was generally guided by sound common sense and practical wisdom. He was more free from arbitrary and fanciful interpretations than any other patristic commentator. He pays proper attention to the connection, and puts himself into the psychological state and historical situation of the writer. In one word, he comes very near to what we now call the grammatico-historical exegesis. This is the only solid and sound foundation for any legitimate use of the Scriptures. The sacred writers had one definite object in view; they wished to convey one particular sense by the ordinary use of language, and to be clearly understood by their readers. At the same time the truths of revelation are so deep and so rich that they can be indefinitely expanded and applied to all circumstances and conditions. Interpretation is one thing, application is another thing. Chrysostom knew as well as any allegorist how to derive spiritual nourishment from the Scriptures and to make them "profitable for teaching, for reproof, for correction, for instruction in righteousness; that the man of God may be complete, thoroughly furnished unto every good work."—As to the text of the Greek Testament, he is the chief witness of the Syro-Constantinopolitan recension, which was followed by the later Greek Fathers. He accepts the Syrian canon of the Peshito, which includes the Old Testament with the Apocrypha, but omits from the New Testament the Apocalypse and four Catholic Epistles (2 Peter, 2 and 3 John, and Jude); at least in the *Synopsis Veteris et novi Testamenti* which is found in his works, these five books are wanting, but this does not prove that he did not know them.

The commentaries of Chrysostom are of unequal merit. We must always remember that he is not a critical but a homiletical and practical commentator who aimed at the conversion and edification of his hearers. He makes frequent digressions, and neglects to explain the difficulties of important texts. Grammatical remarks are rare, but noteworthy on account of his familiarity with the Greek as his mother tongue, though by no means coming up to the accuracy of a modern expert in philology. In the Old Testament he depended altogether on the Septuagint, being ignorant of Hebrew, and often missed the mark. The homilies on the Pauline Epistles are considered his best, especially those to the Corinthians, where he had to deal with moral and pastoral questions. The doctrinal topics of Romans and Galatians were less to his taste, and it cannot be said that he entered into the depths of Paul's doctrines of sin and grace, or ascended the height of his conception of freedom in Christ. His homilies on Romans are argumentative; his continuous notes on Galatians somewhat hasty and superficial. The eighty homilies on Matthew from his Antiochian period are very valuable. Thomas Aquinas declared he would rather possess them than be the master of all Paris. The eighty-eight homilies on John, also preached at Antioch, but to a select audience early in the morning, are more doctrinal and controversial, being directed against the Anomœans (Arians). We have no commentaries from him on Mark and Luke, nor on the Catholic Epistles and the Apocalypse. The fifty-five homilies on the Acts, delivered at Constantinople between Easter and Whitsuntide, when that book was read in the public lessons, contain much interesting information about the manners and customs of the age, but are the least polished of his productions. Erasmus, who translated them into Latin, doubted their genuineness. His life in Constantinople was too much disturbed to leave him quiet leisure for preparation. The homilies on the Hebrews, likewise preached in Constantinople, were published after his death from notes of his friend, the presbyter Constantine, and the text is in a confused state.

The homilies of Chrysostom were a rich storehouse for the Greek commentators, compilers and epitomizers, such as Theodoret, Œcumenius, Theophylact, and Euthymius Zigabenus, and they are worth consulting to this day for their exegetical as well as their practical value.

The theology of Chrysostom must be gathered chiefly from his commentaries. He differs from the metaphysical divines of the Nicene age by his predominantly practical tendency, and in this respect he approaches the genius of the Western Church. He lived between the great trinitarian and christological controversies and was only involved incidentally in the subordinate Origenistic controversy, in which he showed a charitable and liberal spirit. He accepted the Nicene Creed, but he died before the rise of the Nestorian and Eutychian heresies. Speculation was not his forte, and as a thinker he is behind Athanasius, Gregory of Nyssa, and John of Damascus. He was a rhetorician rather than a logician.

Like all the Greek Fathers, he laid great stress on free will and the co-operation of the human will with divine grace in the work of conversion. Cassian, the founder of Semi-Pelagianism, was his pupil and appealed to his authority. Julian of Eclanum, the ablest opponent of Augustin, quoted Chrysostom against original sin; Augustin tried from several passages to prove the reverse, but could only show that Chrysostom was no Pelagian. We may say that in tendency and spirit he was a catholic Semi-Pelagian or Synergist before Semi-Pelagianism was brought into a system.

His anthropology forms a wholesome contrast and supplement to the anthropology of his younger contemporary, the great Bishop of Hippo, the champion of the slavery of the human will and the sovereignty of divine grace.

We look in vain in Chrysostom's writings for the Augustinian and Calvinistic doctrines of a double predestination, total depravity, hereditary guilt, irresistible grace, perseverance of saints, or for the Lutheran theory of forensic and solifidian justification. He teaches that God foreordained all men to holiness and salvation, and that Christ died for all and is both willing and able to save all, but not against their will and without their free consent. The vessels of mercy were prepared by God unto glory, the vessels of wrath were not intended by God, but fitted by their own sin, for destruction. The will of man, though injured by the Fall, has still the power to accept or to reject the offer of salvation. It must first obey the divine call. "When we have begun," he says, in commenting on John i. 38, "when we have sent our will before, then God gives us abundant opportunities of salvation." God helps those who help themselves. "When God," he says, "sees us eagerly prepare for the contest of virtue, He instantly supplies us with His assistance, lightens our labors and strengthens the weakness of our nature." Faith and good works are necessary conditions of justification and salvation, though Christ's merits alone are the efficient cause. He remarks on John vi. 44, that while no man can come to Christ unless drawn and taught by the Father, there is no excuse for those who are unwilling to be thus drawn and taught. Yet, on the other hand, he fully admits the necessity of divine grace at the very beginning of every good action. "We can do no good thing at all," he says, "except we are aided from above." And in his dying hour he gave glory to God "for all things."

Augustinians and Semi-Pelagians, Calvinists and Arminians, widely as they differ in theory about human freedom and divine sovereignty, meet in the common feeling of personal responsibility and absolute dependence on God. With one voice they disclaim all merit of their own and give all glory to Him who is the giver of every good and perfect gift and works in us "both to will and to work, for His good pleasure" (Phil. ii. 12).

As to the doctrines which separate the Greek, Roman, and Protestant churches, Chrysostom faithfully represents the Greek Catholic Church prior to the separation from Rome. In addition to the œcumenical doctrines of the Nicene Creed, he expresses strong views on baptismal regeneration, the real presence, and the eucharistic sacrifice, yet without a clearly defined theory, which was the result of later controversies; hence it would be unjust to press his devotional and rhetorical language into the service of transubstantiation, or consubstantiation, or the Roman view of the mass.

His extravagant laudations of saints and martyrs promoted that refined form of idolatry which in the Nicene age began to take the place of the heathen hero-worship. But it is all the more remarkable that he furnishes no support to Mariolatry, which soon after his death triumphed in the Greek as well as the Latin Church. He was far from the idea of the sinless perfection and immaculate conception of the Virgin Mary. He derives her conduct at the wedding of Cana (John ii. 3, 4) from undue haste and a sort of unholy ambition for the premature display of the miraculous power of her Son; and in commenting on Matthew xii. 46–49, he charges her and the brethren of Christ with vanity and a carnal mind. He does not use the term *theotokos* (bearing God, *Deipara*, Mother of God), which twenty years after his death gave rise to the Nestorian controversy, and which was endorsed by the third and fourth Œcumenical Councils.

As to the question of the papacy he considered the bishop of Rome as the successor of Peter, the prince of the apostles, and appealed to him in his exile against the unjust condemnation of the Council at the Oak. Such appeals furnished the popes a welcome opportunity to act as judges in the controversies of the Easter Church, and greatly strengthened their claims. But his epistle to Innocent was addressed also to the bishops of Milan and Aquileia, and falls far short of the language of submission to an infallible authority. He conceded to the pope merely a primacy of honor ($\pi\rho o\sigma\tau\alpha\sigma\acute{\iota}\alpha$, $\alpha\rho\chi\acute{\eta}$), not a supremacy of jurisdiction. He calls the Bishop of Antioch (Ignatius and Flavian) likewise a successor of Peter, who labored there according to the express testimony of Paul. In commenting on Gal. i. 18, he represents Paul as equal in dignity ($\iota\sigma\acute{o}\tau\iota\mu o\varsigma$) to Peter. He was free from jealousy of Rome, but had he lived during the violent controversies between the patriarch of new Rome and the pope of old Rome, it is not doubtful on which side he would have stood.

In one important point Chrysostom approaches the evangelical theology of the Reformation, his devotion to the Holy Scriptures as the only rule of faith. "There is no topic (says W. P. W. Stephens, his best English biographer) on which he dwells more frequently and earnestly than on the duty of every Christian man and woman to study the Bible ; and what he bade others do, that he did pre-eminently himself." He deemed the reading of the Bible the best means for the promotion of Christian life. A Christian without the knowledge of the Scriptures is to him a workman without tools. Even the sight of the Bible deters from sin, how much more the reading. It purifies and consecrates the soul, it introduces it into the holy of holies and brings it into direct communion with God.

CHAPTER XIII.

CHRYSOSTOM AS A PREACHER.

The crowning merit of Chrysostom is his excellency as a preacher. He is generally and justly regarded as the greatest pulpit orator of the Greek Church. Nor has he any superior or equal among the Latin Fathers. He remains to this day a model for preachers in large cities.

He was trained in the school of Demosthenes and Libanius, and owed much of his literary culture to the classics. He praises "the polish of Isocrates, the gravity of Demosthenes, the dignity of Thucydides, and the sublimity of Plato." He assigns to Plato the first rank among the philosophers, but he places St. Paul far above him, and glories in the victory of the tent-maker and fishermen over the wisdom of the Greeks.

He was not free from the defects of the degenerate rhetoric of his age, especially a flowery exuberance of style and fulsome extravagance in eulogy of dead martyrs and living men. But the defects are overborne by the virtues: the fulness of Scripture knowledge, the intense earnestness, the fruitfulness of illustration and application, the variation of topics, the command of language, the elegance and rhythmic flow of his Greek style, the dramatic vivacity, the quickness and ingenuity of his turns, and the magnetism of sympathy with his hearers. He knew how to draw, in the easiest manner, spiritual nourishment and lessons of practical wisdom from the Word of God, and to make it a divine voice of warning and comfort to every hearer. He was a faithful preacher of truth and righteousness and told fearlessly the whole duty of man. If he was too severe at times, he erred on virtue's side. He preached morals rather than dogmas, Christianity rather than theology, active, practical Christianity that proves itself in holy living and dying. He was a martyr of the pulpit, for it was chiefly his faithful preaching that caused his exile. The effect of his oratory was enhanced by the magnetism of his personality, and is weakened to the reader of a translation or even the Greek original. The living voice and glowing manner are far more powerful than the written and printed letter.

Chrysostom attracted large audiences, and among them many who would rather have gone to the theatre than hear any ordinary preacher. He held them spell-bound to the close. Sometimes they manifested their admiration by noisy applause, and when he rebuked them for it, they would applaud his eloquent rebuke. "You praise," he would tell them, "what I have said, and receive my exhortation with tumults of applause; but show your approbation by obedience; that is the only praise I seek."

The great mediæval poet Dante assigns to Chrysostom a place in Paradise between Nathan the prophet and Anselm the theologian, because, like Nathan, he rebuked the sins of the court, and, like Anselm, he suffered exile for his conviction. The best French pulpit orators—

Bossuet, Massilon, Bourdaloue—have taken him for their model, even in his faults, the flattery of living persons. Villemain praises him as the greatest orator who combined all the attributes of eloquence. Hase calls his eloquence "Asiatic, flowery, full of spirit and of the Holy Spirit, based on sound exegesis, and with steady application to life." English writers compare him to Jeremy Taylor. Gibbon (who confesses, however, to have read very few of his homilies) attributes to him "the happy art of engaging the passions in the service of virtue, and of exposing the folly as well as the turpitude of vice, almost with the truth and spirit of a dramatic representation." Dean Milman describes him as an "unrivalled master in that rapid and forcible application of incidental occurrences which gives such life and reality to eloquence. He is at times, in the highest sense, dramatic in manner." Stephens, in his excellent biography, thus characterizes his sermons: "A power of exposition which unfolded in lucid order, passage by passage, the meaning of the book in hand; a rapid transition from clear exposition, or keen logical argument, to fervid exhortation, or pathetic appeal, or indignant denunciation; the versatile ease with which he could lay hold of any little incident of the moment, such as the lighting of the lamps in the church, and use it to illustrate his discourse; the mixture of plain common sense, simple boldness, and tender affection, with which he would strike home to the hearts and consciences of his hearers—all these are not only general characteristics of the man, but are usually to be found manifested more or less in the compass of each discourse. It is this rare union of powers which constitutes his superiority to almost all other Christian preachers with whom he might be, or has been, compared. Savonarola had all, and more than all, his fire and vehemence, but untempered by his sober, calm good sense, and wanting his rational method of interpretation. Chrysostom was eager and impetuous at times in speech as well as in action, but never fanatical. Jeremy Taylor combines, like Chrysostom, real earnestness of purpose with rhetorical forms of expression and florid imagery; but, on the whole, his style is far more artificial, and is overlaid with a multifarious learning, from which Chrysostom's was entirely free. Wesley is almost his match in simple, straightforward, practical exhortation, but does not rise into flights of eloquence like his. The great French preachers, again, resemble him in his more ornate and declamatory vein, but they lack that simpler common-sense style of address which equally distinguished him."

I conclude this sketch with the eloquent tribute of Archdeacon Farrar (in his recent work, *Lives of the Fathers*, 1889): "John Chrysostom is one of the most splendid and interesting figures in the early history of the Church. Less profound a theologian than Athanasius, or Augustin, or Gregory of Nazianzen; less independent a thinker than Theodore of Mopsuestia; less learned than Origen or Jerome; less practically successful than Ambrose, he yet combines so many brilliant gifts that he stands almost supreme among the *Doctores Ecclesiæ*, as an orator, as an exegete, as a great moral reformer, as a saint and confessor who,

> 'For the testimony of truth has borne
> Universal reproach, far worse to bear
> Than violence; for this was all his care
> To stand approved in sight of God, though worlds
> Judged him perverse.'

"The general purity and practical wholesomeness of his doctrines, the loftiness of his moral standard, the indomitable courage of his testimony against the vices of all classes, the glory of his oratory, the prominent position which he occupied in his own generation, the tragedy and failure of his life, surround his name with a halo as bright as that of any of the great ecclesiastical leaders of the early centuries. He was the ideal preacher to the great capital of the world."

LITERATURE.

For a list of the literature on St. Chrysostom, the reader is referred to Schaff's *History of the Christian Church* (last revision, 1889), vol. III., 933 and 1036 sq., and his *Nicene and Post-Nicene Library*, First Series (1889), vol. IX., 3-5.

The best edition of St. Chrysostom's Works is the Benedictine of BERNARD DE MONTFAUCON, Greek and Latin, Paris, 1718-38, in 13 vols. fol., reprinted with various improvements by Gaume, Paris, 1834-39, and in Migne's *Patrologia Græca*, 1859-63. The best critical edition of the Greek text of the Homilies on Matthew and the Pauline Epistles is by Dr. FREDERICK FIELD, Cambridge and Oxford, 1839-62, in 7 vols. The English edition has already been mentioned, p. 41.

The best biographers of St. Chrysostom are NEANDER in German (*Der heil. Chrysostomus*, 1821, 3d ed., Berlin, 1848, 2 vols.), and W. R. W. STEPHENS in English (*St. Chrysostom, his Life and Times*, 1872, 3d ed., London, 1883). The present sketch is substantially the same as that contained in the author's Prolegomena to his edition of St. Chrysostom's works.

SAINT AUGUSTIN.

SAINT AUGUSTIN.

"Thou, O God, hast made us for Thee, and our heart is restless until it rests in Thee."

INTRODUCTORY.

The chief, almost the only source of the life of St. Augustin till the time of his conversion is his autobiography; his faithful friend, Possidius, added a few notices; his public labors till his death are recorded in his numerous writings; his influence is written on the pages of mediæval and modern church history.

Among religious autobiographies the *Confessions* of Augustin still hold the first rank. In them this remarkable man, endowed with a lofty genius and a burning heart, lays open his inner life before God and the world, and at the same time the life of God in his own soul, which struggled for the mastery, and at last obtained it. A more honest book was never written. He conceals nothing, he palliates nothing. Like a faithful witness against himself, standing at the bar of the omniscient Judge, he tells the truth, the whole truth, and nothing but the truth. Like King David, in the fifty-first Psalm, he openly confesses his transgressions with unfeigned sorrow and grief, yet in the joyous consciousness of forgiveness. To his sense of sin corresponds his sense of grace: they are the controlling ideas of his spiritual life and of his system of theology. The deeper the descent into the hell of self-knowledge, the higher the ascent to the knowledge of God.

Augustin might have kept the secret of his youthful aberrations; posterity knows them only from his pen.

He committed no murder nor adultery, like the King of Israel; he never denied his Saviour, like Peter; he was no persecutor of the Church, like Paul; his sins preceded his conversion and baptism, and they were compatible with the highest honor in heathen society. But his Christian experience quickened his sense of guilt, and he told the story for his own humiliation and for the glory of God's redeeming grace.

The *Confessions* are a solemn soliloquy before the throne of the Searcher of hearts within the hearing of the world. They enter into the deepest recesses of religious experience, and rise to the lofty summit of theological thought. They exhibit a mind intensely pious and at the same time intensely speculative. His prayers are meditations, and his meditations are prayers; and both shine and burn like Africa's tropical sun. They reflect, as Guizot says, "a unique mixture of passion and gentleness, of authority and sympathy, of largeness of mind and logical rigor." Dr. Shedd ranks them among those rare autobiographies in which "the ordinary experiences of human life attain to such a pitch of intensity and such a breadth, range, and depth as to strike the reader with both a sense of familiarity and a sense of strangeness. It is his own human thought and human feeling that he finds expressed; and yet it is spoken with so much greater clearness, depth, and energy than he is himself capable of, or than is characteristic of the mass of men, that it seems like the experience of another sphere and another race of beings." *

Even in a psychological and literary point of view the *Confessions* of Augustin rank among the most interest-

---

* See the thoughtful introduction to his edition of the *Confessions of Augustin*, Andover, 1860, p. ix.

ing of autobiographies, and are not inferior to Rousseau's *Confessions* and Goethe's *Truth and Fiction;* while in religious value there is no comparison between them. They are equally frank, and blend the personal with the general human interest; but while the French philosopher and the German poet are absorbed in the analysis of their own self, and dwell upon it with satisfaction, the African father goes into the minute details of his sins and follies with intense abhorrence of sin, and rises above himself to the contemplation of divine mercy, which delivered him from the degrading slavery. The former wrote for the glory of man, the latter for the glory of God. Augustin lived in an age when the Western Roman Empire was fast approaching dissolution, and the Christian Church, the true City of God, was being built on its ruins. He was not free from the defects of an artificial and degenerate rhetoric; nevertheless he rises not seldom to the height of passionate eloquence, and scatters gems of the rarest beauty. He was master of the antithetical power, the majesty and melody of the language of imperial Rome. Many of his sentences have passed into proverbial use, and become commonplaces in theological literature.

Next to Augustin himself, his mother attracts the attention and excites the sympathy of the reader. She walks like a guardian angel from heaven through his book until her translation to that sphere. How pure and strong and enduring her devotion to him, and his devotion to her! She dried many tears of anxious mothers. It is impossible to read of Monnica without a profounder regard for woman and a feeling of gratitude for Christianity, which raised her to so high a position.

The *Confessions* were written about A.D. 397, ten years after Augustin's conversion. The historical part closes with his conversion and with the death of his mother. The work contains much that can be fully understood only by the theologian and the student of history; and the last four of the thirteen books are devoted to subtle speculations about the nature of memory, eternity, time, and creation, which far transcend the grasp of the ordinary reader. Nevertheless it was read with great interest and profit in the time of the writer, and ever since, in the original Latin and numerous translations in various languages. In all that belongs to elevation, depth, and emotion there are few books so edifying and inspiring and so well worthy of careful study as Augustin's *Confessions*.

We shall endeavor to popularize the *Confessions*, and to supplement the biography from other sources, for the instruction and edification of the present generation. The life of a great genius and saint like Augustin is one of the best arguments for the religion he professed, and to which he devoted his mental and moral energies.

St. Augustin had no other force but that of intellect and piety. And yet he exerted more influence than any pope or emperor in the history of Christianity. Africa relapsed into barbarism after his death, but Europe was educated by his spirit. He has written his name indelibly on every page of the Middle Ages and of the Reformation. He was the teacher of Anselm and Thomas Aquinas, of St. Bernard and Thomas à Kempis, of Wiclif and Hus, of Luther and Calvin, of Jansen and Pascal. He furnished the programme for the papal theocracy, and aided in its dissolution; he struck the key-note of scholasticism and mysticism; he instructed the Reformers in the mysteries of sin and grace, and led them to the abyss of eternal predestination. Even now, fifteen hundred years after his conversion, his theological opinions carry more weight in the Catholic and Evangelical Churches than those of any other uninspired man, and are likely to do so till God sends a teacher who will descend deeper and ascend higher than Augustin in the exploration of the mysteries of divine truth.

Quite recently Dr. Adolf Harnack, who sits in Neander's chair of Church History in Berlin, has given an admiring estimate of the amazing influence of the Bishop of Hippo.* He has also published a suggestive essay on the *Confessions of Augustin*,† in which he draws an ingenious parallel between him and Goethe's *Faust*. But the main points in the former—repentance and conversion—are wanting in the latter. Faust became disgusted with the world after enjoying its pleasures, and regretted the consequences of his sins, but did not repent of sin itself. He is carried down to hell by Mephistopheles in the first part of Goethe's tragedy, but he reappears in heaven in the second part, without any moral change except that brought about by his own exertion and the attraction of the "ever-womanly," which is the symbol of divine grace. In Augustin grace is not an outward help merely (as with Pelagius and Goethe), but a regenerating and sanctifying power without which man can do nothing.

---

* In the third volume of his *Lehrbuch der Dogmengeschichte*, Freiburg i. B., 1890.

† *Augustin's Confessionen. Ein Vortrag.* Giessen, 1888.

SAINT AUGUSTIN.

CHAPTER I.

AUGUSTIN'S YOUTH.

AURELIUS AUGUSTINUS, the greatest and best, and the most influential of the Latin church-fathers, was born on the thirteenth of November, 354, at Tagaste, in Numidia, North Africa. His birthplace was near Hippo Regius (now Bona), where he spent his public life as presbyter and bishop, and where he died in the seventy-sixth year of his age (Aug. 28, 430). He belonged to the Punic race, which was of Phœnician origin, but became Latinized in language, laws, and customs under Roman rule since the destruction of Carthage (B.C. 146), yet retained the Oriental temper and the sparks of the genius of Hannibal, the sworn enemy of Rome. These traits appear in the writings of Tertullian and Cyprian, who preceded Augustin and prepared the way for his theology. In Augustin we can trace the religious intensity of the Semitic race, the tropical fervor of Africa, the Catholic grasp and comprehensiveness of Rome, and the germs of an evangelical revolt against its towering ambition and tyrannical rule. His native land has long since been laid waste by the barbarous Vandals (A.D. 439) and the Mohammedan Arabs (647), and keeps mournful silence over dreary ruins; but his spirit marched through the ages, and still lives and acts as a molding and stimulating power in all the branches of Western Christendom.

His father, Patricius, was a member of the city Council, and a man of kindly disposition, but irritable temper and dissolute habits. He remained a heathen till shortly before his death, but did not, as it appears, lay any obstruction to the Christian course of his wife.

Monnica,* the mother of Augustin, shines among the most noble and pious women that adorn the grand temple of the Christian Church. She was born in the year 331 or 332, of Christian parents, probably at Tagaste. She had rare gifts of mind and heart, which were developed by an excellent Christian education, and dedicated to the Saviour. To the violent passion of her husband she opposed an angelic meekness, and when the outburst was over she reproached him so tenderly that he was always shamed. Had the rebuke been administered sooner it would only have fed the unhallowed fire. His conjugal infidelity she bore with patience and forgiving love. Her highest aim was to win him over to the Christian faith—not so much by words as by a truly humble and godly conduct and the conscientious discharge of her household duties. In this she was so successful that, a year before his death, he enrolled himself among the catechumens and was baptized. To her it was the greatest pleasure to read the Holy Scriptures

---

* This is the correct spelling, according to the oldest MSS. of the writings of Augustin, and is followed by Pusey, in his edition of the *Confessions*, by Moule, in Smith and Wace, *Dict. of Christian Biography*, III. 932, and also by K. Braune, in *Monnika und Augustinus* (Grimma, 1846). The usual spelling is *Monica*, in French *Monique*. It is derived by some from μόνος, *single;* by others from μόννος or ιάννος, Lat. *monile, a necklace* (*monilia, jewels*).

and to attend church regularly every morning and evening, "not," as Augustin says, "to listen to vain fables, but to the Lord, in the preaching of His servants, and to offer up to Him her prayers." She esteemed it a precious privilege to lay on the altar each day a gift of love, to bestow alms on the poor, and to extend hospitality to strangers, especially to brethren in the faith. She brought up her children in the nurture and admonition of the Lord. She bare Augustin, as he boasts of her, with greater pains spiritually than she had brought him forth naturally into the world.* For thirty years she prayed for the conversion of her distinguished son, until at last, a short time before her death, after manifold cares and burning tears, in the midst of which she never either murmured against God or lost hope, she found her prayers answered beyond her expectations. She has become a bright example and rich comfort for mothers, and will act as an inspiration to the end of time.

From such parents sprang Augustin. Strong sensual passions he inherited from his father, but from his mother those excellent gifts of mind and heart which, though long perverted, were at last reclaimed by the regenerating grace of God, and converted into an incalculable blessing to the Church of all ages. He had a brother, by the name of Navigius, a widowed sister, who presided over a society of pious women till the day of her death, and a number of nephews and nieces.

Augustin says that with his mother's milk his heart sucked in the name of the Saviour, which became so

---

* *Confess.* l. V. c. 9 : " *Non enim satis eloquor, quid erga me habebat animi, et quanto majore sollicitudine me parturiebat spiritu, quam carne pepererat.*" Likewise l. IX. c. 8 : " *Quae me parturivit, et carne, ut in hanc temporalem, et corde, ut in aeternam lucem nascerer.*" Comp. his whole description of Monnica, ix. 9–12.

firmly lodged there that nothing which did not savor of that name, however learned and attractive it might otherwise be, could ever fully charm him. He early lisped out prayers to God, whose all-embracing love revealed itself to his childish spirit. These germs of piety were overgrown by the weeds of youthful vice and impure lusts, but never wholly smothered. Even in the midst of his furthest wanderings he still heard the low, sad echo of his youthful religious impressions, was attended by the guardian genius of his praying mother, and felt in the depths of his noble spirit the pulse-beat of that strong desire after God, to which, in the opening of his *Confessions*, he gives utterance in the incomparable words: " Thou, O God, hast created us for Thyself, and our heart is without rest, until it rests in Thee." *

He was not baptized in infancy, but merely offered to the initiation of a catechumen by the sign of the cross and the salting with salt.† There was at that time no compulsory baptism of infants: it was left to the free choice of the parents. Monnica probably shared the view of Tertullian that it was safer to postpone baptism to years of discretion than to run the risk of forfeiting its benefit by a relapse.

Augustin was sent to school at an early age, with the hope on the part of his father that he might become distinguished in the world; on that of his mother, that

---

* *Confess.* I. 1 : "*Fecisti nos ad Te, et inquietum est cor nostrum, donec requiescat in Te.*" Dr. Pusey, in his translation (based on an older one), obliterates the paronomasia—*inquietum, requiescat*: "Thou madest us for Thyself, and our heart is *restless*, until it *repose* in Thee." Dr. Shedd retains this translation.

† *Confess.* I. 11.

"the common studies might not only prove innocent, but also in some degree useful in leading him afterward to God."

Elementary instruction and mathematics were, however, too dry for the boy; and he was, in consequence, severely punished by his teachers. Play was his chief delight. In order to shine as the first among his companions he even cheated them; and for the purpose of providing himself with playthings, or of gratifying his appetite, he went so far as to steal from the store-room and the table of his parents. At public shows he passionately crowded himself into the front ranks of the spectators.

And yet for all this he had to endure the reproaches of conscience. On one occasion, when, seized by a violent cramp in the stomach, he believed his last hour had come, he earnestly begged to be baptized. But after his mother had made the necessary preparations he suddenly grew better, and the baptism, according to a prevailing notion of the age, was postponed, lest this precious means for the washing away of past sins might be rendered vain by the contraction of new guilt, in which case no other remedy was to be found. At a later period he thought it would have been far better for him had he been early received by baptism into the communion of the Church, and thus placed under her protecting care.

His dislike for learning ceased when Augustin passed over from rudimentary studies into the grammar school. The poet Vergil charmed his fancy and filled him with fresh enthusiasm. With the deepest interest he followed Æneas in his wanderings, and shed tears over the death of Dido, who slew herself for love; while at the same time, as he tells us, he ought to have mourned over his own death in estrangement from God.* The wooden horse full of armed warriors, the burning of Troy, and the shade of Creusa were continually before his soul. The Grecian classics were not so much to his taste, because his defective knowledge of the language, which he never had the patience to master, prevented the enjoyment of their works.

By his gift of lively representation and brilliant oratorical talent he made a figure in the school, and awakened the fondest hopes in the hearts of his parents. His father destined him to the then highly respectable and influential office of rhetorician, or public teacher of forensic eloquence. For further improvement he sent him to the larger neighboring city of Madaura, where heathenism still held almost exclusive sway. His residence there was probably injurious to him in a moral point of view.

In the sixteenth year of his age he returned home in order to prepare himself, in as cheap a manner as possible, for the University of the metropolis of Northern Africa. But instead of growing better he entered upon the path of folly, and plunged into the excesses of sensuality. His mother earnestly exhorted him to lead a chaste life; but he was ashamed to heed the exhortation of a woman. This false shame drove him even to pretend frequently to crimes which he had never committed, so as not to seem to fall behind his comrades. He himself confesses, "I was not able to distinguish the brighter purity of love from the darkness of lust. Both

---

* *Confess.* I. 13 : " *Quid enim miserius misero non miserante seipsum, et flente Didonis mortem, quæ fiebat amando Æneam; non flente autem mortem suam, quæ fiebat non amando Te, Deus lumen cordis mei, et panis oris intus animæ meæ, et virtus maritans mentem meam, et sinum cogitationis meæ?*"

were mingled together in confusion ; youth in its weakness, hurried to the abyss of desire, was swallowed up in the pool of vice."

Yet, amid these wild impulses, it was not well with him. That longing after God, so deeply rooted in his soul, asserted its power again and again. He became more and more discontented with himself, and after every indulgence felt an inward pang. The guiding hand of the Lord mixed in the cup of his enjoyment " the wholesome bitterness that leads us back from destructive pleasure, by which we are estranged from God."

CHAPTER II.

AUGUSTIN AT CARTHAGE.

In his seventeenth year, the same in which his father died, he entered the High School of Carthage, supported by his mother and the richest citizen of Tagaste, Romanianus, who was a distant relative. Carthage was the Rome of Africa, with many marble palaces, numerous schools, countless shows, and shameless vices. Monnica did not see her son depart for the great and voluptuous city without fear and trembling, but she was not willing now to interrupt his career, and she knew Him who is stronger than all temptation, and listens to the prayers of His children. In Carthage Augustin studied oratory and other sciences, astrology even, and raised himself to the first rank by his talent. This increased his ambition and fed his pride.

With his morals he fared badly. He consorted with a

class of students who sought their honor in deriding good conduct, and called themselves "Destroyers." Although their rough and vulgar doings were peculiarly disagreeable to a nature so noble as his, yet their society must have exerted over him a pernicious influence. He frequently visited also the tragic theatre, because it was always, says he, "filled with pictures of my misery, and tinder for my desires."

In his eighteenth year he took up with a woman, with whom he lived thirteen years without marriage, and was faithful to her. She bore him a son, Adeodatus, whose promising gifts gave his father much joy, but he died at an early age. She walks veiled through the *Confessions*, a memory without a name, and disappears with a sigh of repentance and a vow to devote herself to a pure and single life.

It should be borne in mind that the excesses of his youth are known to us only from his own honest *Confessions*. His worst sin was common in the best heathen society, and sanctioned by the Roman law. It did not in the least affect his respectability in the eyes of the world. Even the Emperor Marcus Aurelius, the model saint and philosopher of ancient Rome, kept a concubine after the death of his wife, without feeling the least scruple. Tertullian, Cyprian, Jerome, and other eminent fathers who embraced Christianity in adult years, were probably no better than Augustin before his conversion, but they left only vague allusions. Augustin never was a profligate. He was strictly faithful to the one woman of his affection, the first from Africa, the second from Italy.[*] It is therefore an inexcusable slander to call him "the

---

[*] *Confess.* IV. 2 : "*In illis annis unam habebam, . . . sed unam tamen, ei quoque servans tori fidem.*" Comp. VI. 15.

promiscuous lover of the frail beauties of Carthage." It was wicked and brutal in Byron to write that Saint Augustin's "fine *Confessions* make the reader envy his transgressions." The wisdom of some parts of his *Confessions* may be doubted, but they were made to impress the reader with his own intense abhorrence of sin, and we must admire the fearless honesty and keen moral sensibility of the man in revealing the secrets of his former life, which otherwise would never have been known.

CHAPTER III.

CICERO'S HORTENSIUS.

MEANWHILE, beneath this rushing stream of external activity, the soul of Augustin sighed after true wisdom. His ardent thirst for something ideal and enduring first of all showed itself in the study of the *Hortensius* of Cicero, which came up regularly in the course of his education. This lost volume contained an encouragement to true philosophy, and gave the direction, in its study, to aim at truth only, and, above all, to hail her footsteps with enthusiasm and without regard to the interest of party. This roused the young man to an earnest struggle after truth.

"This book," says he, "transformed my inclinations and turned my prayers to Thee, O God, and changed my wishes and my desires. Every vain hope was extinguished; and I longed, with an incredible fervor of spirit, after the immortality of wisdom. I began to raise myself that I might return to Thee. I studied this book again and again, not for the refinement of my language nor for aid in the art of speaking, but in order that I might be persuaded by its doctrine. Oh, how I burned, my God—how I burned to fly back from the things of earth to Thee. And I knew not what Thou hadst designed with me. For with Thee is wisdom, and these writings excited me toward love, toward wisdom, toward philosophy. And this particularly delighted me, that I was not asked therein to love, to seek, to attain, and to hold in firm embrace this or that school—but wisdom alone, as she might reveal herself. I was charmed and inflamed."

But the volume contained one blemish: the name of Christ was not there. Such a secret power did that name, imprinted on his tender soul, exert over him, even during his wanderings.

In this thirst after truth he laid hold of the records of revelation—that holy book to which his mother clung with such reverent devotion. But there was yet a great gulf fixed between him and the Bible. In order to be understood it requires an humble, childlike disposition. To the proud in spirit it is a book with seven seals. The natural man perceives not the things that belong to the Spirit of God: they are foolishness unto him, because they are spiritually discerned. Augustin was not yet acquainted with the depth of his corruption, which the Holy Scriptures disclosed to him on every page. "The Scriptures," he says, "thrive among the childlike; but I refused to become a child, and thought myself great in my own presumption." He desired not truth in her simple beauty, but arrayed in a specious garb of rhetoric, to flatter his vanity; he desired her not as a chaste virgin, but as a voluptuous courtesan.

Hence he now turned to the sect of the Manichæans,

who had the word truth always on their lips, but held their disciples captive in the bondage of error.

CHAPTER IV.

AUGUSTIN AMONG THE MANICHÆANS.

The Manichæans, so called from their founder, the Persian Mani, or Manichæus (died 274), were a sect allied to the Gnostics. They blended together heathenism and Christianity in a fantastic system, which they set up in opposition to Judaism and the Catholic Church. The groundwork of their doctrine is the Old Persian religion, into which a few Christian elements are introduced in a distorted form. They were dualists; they taught, as Zoroaster, an original antagonism between God and matter; between the kingdom of light and the kingdom of darkness; between good and evil. Man stands in the middle between both these kingdoms; he has a spark of light in him which longs after redemption, but, at the same time, is possessed of a corrupt body and a corrupt soul, which are to be gradually annihilated. To a certain degree they acknowledged Christ as a Saviour, but confounded Him with the sun; for they were accustomed to drag down the spiritual ideas of the gospel into the sphere of natural life. In the entire economy of nature, which, along with the perfume of the flower, sends the miasmatic breath, and causes the gloomy night to succeed the clear day, they saw a conflict between the two opposite kingdoms; in every plant a crucified Christ, an imprisoned spirit of light, which worked itself up from the dark bosom of the earth and strove toward the sun. The class of the *perfect* among them durst slay or wound no animal, pluck no flower, break no stalk of grass, for fear of injuring the higher spirit dwelling in it. They regarded the whole Catholic Church as contaminated by Judaistic elements. Mani is the Paraclete or Advocate promised by Christ, who is to restore again the true Church. They reproached the orthodox Christians for believing blindly, on mere authority, and for not elevating themselves to the standpoint of independent knowledge. They, the Manichæans, thought themselves, on the contrary, in the possession of perfect knowledge, of truth in her pure, unveiled form. The words truth, science, reason, never out of their mouths, were esteemed as excellent baits for strangers.

These lofty pretensions and promises to unravel all the riddles of existence, the longing after redemption, characteristic of the system, its inward sympathy with the life of nature, the dazzling show of its subtle dialectics and polemics against the doctrines of the church, and the ascetic severity of its course of life, explain the attractive power which the Manichæan philosophy exerted over many of the more profound spirits of the age, and the extensive propagation which it met with even in the West.

We can readily imagine how Augustin, taken up with his struggles after truth, but at the same time full of intellectual pride, as he then was, should be won over by its delusive charms. He enrolled himself in the class of the *auditors*, or catechumens. His mother mourned over this new aberration, but was consoled by a dream, in which a shining youth told her that her son should stand just where she stood. When she informed her son of it, he interpreted the dream as implying the speedy conversion of his mother to his side. "No, no," answered she, "it was not said to me, where he is there shalt thou be also; but, where thou art, there shall he be also." Augustin confesses that this prompt reply made a greater impression on him than the dream itself. She was likewise comforted by a bishop, who, at a former period, had been himself a Manichæan. She begged him to convince her son of his error. But he thought disputation would be of no avail. She should only continue to pray for him, and gradually, of his own accord, through study and experience, he would come to a clearer understanding. "As sure as you live," he added, "it is not possible that a son of such tears should be lost." Monnica treasured up these words as a prophetic voice from heaven.

For nine years, up to the twenty-eighth of his life, Augustin remained in connection with these heretics— led astray, and leading others astray. Their discovery of seeming contradictions in the doctrines of the Church, their polemics against the Old Testament, their speculations concerning the origin of evil, which they traced back to a primordial principle co-existent with God Himself, spoke to his understanding, while their symbolical interpretations of the varied aspects of nature addressed his lively imagination.

And yet, for all this, the deepest want of his reason remained unsatisfied. At the time of the high church festivals particularly, when all Christians flocked to the services of the altar, in order to die with the Lord on Good Friday, and rise again with Him on Easter morning, he was seized with a strong desire after their communion. For this reason he took no step toward entering the higher class of the initiated, or *elect*, among the

Manichæans, but devoted himself more zealously to those studies which belonged to his calling as a rhetorician.

CHAPTER V.

THE LOSS OF A FRIEND.

AFTER the completion of his course of study he returned to Tagaste, in order to settle there as a teacher of rhetoric. He was master of every qualification for inspiring his scholars with enthusiasm, and many of them, especially Alypius, adhered to him through life with the most heartfelt gratitude.

About this time he lost a very dear friend, who, with an almost feminine susceptibility, had resigned himself to the commanding power of his creative intellect, and had even followed him into the mazes of Manichæism. He was suddenly prostrated by a fever. Baptism was administered to him without his knowledge; Augustin, who was with him night and day, made a mock of it. But his friend, when he again became conscious, withstood him with an independence that he had never before exhibited. The empty shadow of a Christ, the sun, the moon, the air, and whatever else was pointed out by Manichæism to the soul thirsting after salvation, could now yield him no comfort—but the simple, childlike faith of the Catholic Church alone. In this faith he departed, when the fever returned with renewed violence.

The death of this friend filled Augustin with inexpressible anguish. Neither the splendor of light, nor the peaceful innocence of the flowers, nor the joys of the banquet, nor the pleasures of sense, had any interest for him now; even his books, for a long while, lost their charms. "Everything I looked upon was death. My fatherland became a torment to me—my father's house a scene of the deepest suffering. Above all, my eyes sought after him; but he was not given back to me again. I hated everything because he was not there. I had become a great enigma to myself."

He afterward saw how wrong it was to place such unbounded dependence on the creature. "Oh, the folly," he laments, "of not knowing how to love men as men! Oh, foolish man, to suffer what is human beyond due measure, as I then did!" "Blessed is he, O Lord, who loves Thee," are his inimitable words, "and his friend in Thee, and his enemy for Thy sake. He alone loses no dear ones, to whom all are dear in Him, who can never be lost to us. And who is He, but our God, the God who made heaven and earth, and fills them all! No one loses Thee but he who forsakes Thee." *

And yet we see in this uncontrollable anguish what a deep fountain of love was gushing in his bosom. Could this love only find its proper object, and be purified by the Spirit of God, what a rich ornament and source of blessing must it become to the Church and the world! At the same time this severe suffering reveals the internal weakness of the Manichæan dogmas and of mere human wisdom. Their consolations cannot reach into the dark hours of trouble; their promises are convicted

---

* *Confess.* IV. 9 : " *Beatus qui amat Te, et amicum in Te, et inimicum propter Te. Solus enim nullum carum amittit, cui omnes in illo cari sunt, qui non amittitur. Et quis est iste, nisi Deus noster, Deus qui fecit cœlum et terram, et implet ea, quia implendo ea fecit ea? Te nemo amittit, nisi qui dimittit; et qui dimittit, quo it, aut quo fugit, nisi a Te placido ad* **Te** *iratum?*"

of falsehood at the brink of the grave. It is true, indeed, that this visitation to his soul passed by without waking him up from his sleep of sin. Still, the death-bed of his friend, which he could not banish from his memory, had certainly the effect of undermining his faith in the Manichæan system.

CHAPTER VI.

AUGUSTIN LEAVES MANICHÆISM.

In consequence of this loss, which embittered his life in his native city, and impelled also by an ambitious desire for a distinguished career, Augustin went back to Carthage, and opened there a school of forensic eloquence. Amid new relationships and in the society of new friends his wounds were gradually healed, and he went forward in his accustomed path with success, though at times the recklessness of the students gave him great pain.

He appeared also as an author, and published a large philosophical work on *Fitness and Beauty.**

For some time yet he adhered to Manichæism, until at last, in his twenty-ninth year, a crisis arrived. By degrees many doubts had arisen in his mind concerning the system. His confidence in the boasted sanctity of the Manichæan priesthood, the class of the *elect*, was shaken by the rumor of secret vices, which held sway among them, under the hypocritical mask of peculiar, ascetic

---

* *De Apto et Pulchro.*

virtues. By the thorough study of philosophy he was able to gain an insight into the many contradictions and untenable points of Manichæan speculation. The notion of evil as a substance co-eternal with God could not satisfy his mind in its struggle after unity.

The Manichæans were unable to solve his doubts, and instead of attempting it, promised to introduce him to their famous bishop, Faustus, who was then regarded as their oracle. He lived at Mileve, a city in the northwestern part of Numidia. Augustin himself was very desirous of becoming acquainted with him. This honor was at last granted. They met in Carthage. He discovered in him a brilliant orator and a subtle dialectician, but at the same time a man of moderate culture and without any depth or earnestness of spirit. He compares him to a cup-bearer who, with graceful politeness, presents a costly goblet without anything in it. "With such things," says he, in allusion to his discourses, "my ears are already satiated. They did not appear better because beautifully spoken, nor true because eloquent, nor spiritually wise because the look was expressive and the discourse select. Thou, my God, hast taught me, in wonderful and hidden ways, that a thing should not seem true because portrayed with eloquence, nor false because the breath of the lips is not sounded according to the rules of art; on the other hand, that a thing is not necessarily true because conveyed in rude, nor false because conveyed in brilliant, language; but that wisdom and folly are like wholesome and noxious viands—both may be contained in tasteful or unadorned words, as they in rough or finely-wrought vessels." In the private conversations which he held with Faustus the latter could not answer questions of vital importance to the truth of the Manichæan system, and was obliged to resort to the Socratic confession of ignorance. But that did not agree well with the intellectual arrogance of this sect.

Now, after their boasted champion had so sadly disappointed his expectations, Augustin resolved on breaking with the heresy, although he did not yet formally renounce his place among its adherents.

CHAPTER VII.

ERROR OVERRULED FOR TRUTH.

Before we go on with our church-father let us take a glance at the connection between his wanderings and his later activity in the Church. The marvellous wisdom of God reveals itself in bringing good out of evil and making even the sins and errors of His servants contribute to their own sanctification and an increase of their usefulness. "He overrules the wrath of men for His glory." David's double crime followed by his repentance, Peter's denial wiped out by his bitter tears, Paul's persecuting zeal turned into apostolic devotion, have been an unfailing source of comfort and encouragement to Christians in their struggle with temptation and sin. And yet by no means does this render wickedness excusable. To the question, "Shall we continue in sin that grace may abound?" the Apostle Paul answers with horror, "God forbid!"

The wild, reckless life of Augustin prepared him to look afterward, in the light of grace, far down into the abyss of sin—into the thorough corruption and ingratitude of the human heart. The bare thought of it must have deeply troubled him, but the humility that can say with Paul, "I am the chief of sinners," is one of the most beautiful pearls in the crown of the Christian character, while spiritual pride and self-righteousness gnaw like worms at the root of piety. There is no church-father who, in regard to deep, unfeigned humility, bears so much resemblance, or stands so near to the great apostle of the Gentiles as Augustin. He manifests in all his writings a noble renunciation of self in the presence of the Most Holy, and his spirit goes forth in thankfulness to the superabounding grace which, in spite of his unworthiness, had drawn him up out of the depths of corruption and overwhelmed him with mercy.

By his own painful experience he was also fitted to develop the doctrine of sin, with such rare penetration and subtlety, to refute the superficial theories of Pelagius, and thus to render an invaluable service to theology and the Church. Further, his theoretical aberration into Manichæism fitted him to overthrow this false and dangerous system, and to prove, by a striking example, how fruitless the search after truth must be outside of the simple, humble faith in Christ. Thus also was St. Paul, by his learned Pharisaic education, better qualified than any other apostle for contending successfully against the false exegesis and legal righteousness of his Judaistic opponents.

CHAPTER VIII.

AUGUSTIN A SCEPTIC IN ROME.

AFTER Augustin had lost faith in Manichæism he found himself in the same situation as he was ten years before. There was the same longing after truth, but linked now with a feeling of desolation, a bitter sense of deception, and a large measure of scepticism. He was no longer at ease in Carthage. He hankered after new associations, new scenes, new fountains out of which to drink the good so ardently desired.

This disposition of mind, in connection with a dislike for the rudeness of the Carthaginian students and the exactions of friends, made him resolve on a journey to Rome, where he ventured to hope for a yet more brilliant and profitable career as a rhetorician. Thus he drew nigher to the place where his inward change was to be decided.

He endeavored to conceal his resolution from his mother, who in the mean time had joined him at Carthage. But she found out something about it, and wished either to prevent him from going, or to go with him.

Augustin would listen to neither proposal, and resorted to a trick to carry out his plan. One evening, in the year 383, he went down to the sea-shore, in order to take ship, near the place where two chapels had been dedicated to the memory of the great church-father and martyr, St. Cyprian. His mother suspected his design, and followed him. He pretended that he merely wished to visit a friend on board, and remain with him until his departure. As she was not satisfied with this explanation, and unwilling to turn back alone, he insisted on her spending at least that one night in the church of the martyr, and then he would come for her.

While she was there in tears, praying and wrestling with God to prevent his voyage, Augustin sailed for the coasts of Italy, and his deceived mother found herself the next morning alone on the shore of the sea. She had learned, however, the heavenly art of forgiving, and believing also, where she could not see. In quiet resignation she returned to the city, and continued to pray for the salvation of her son, waiting the time when the hand of Supreme Wisdom would solve the dark riddle. Though meaning well, she this time erred in her prayer, for the journey of Augustin was the means of his salvation. The denial of the prayer was, in fact, the answering of it. Instead of the form, God granted rather the substance of her petition in the conversion of her son. "Therefore," says he—"therefore hadst Thou, O God, regard to the *aim* and *essence* of her desires, and didst not do what she *then* prayed for, that Thou mightest do for me what she *continually* implored."

After a prosperous voyage across the Mediterranean Augustin found lodging in Rome with a Manichæan host, of the class of the *auditors*, and mingled in the society of the *elect*. He was soon attacked, in the house of this heretic, by a disease brought on and aggravated by the agonies of his soul, dissatisfaction with his course of life, homesickness, and remorse for the heartless deception practised on his mother. The fever rose so high that signs of approaching dissolution had already appeared, and yet Providence had reserved him for a long and active life. "Thou, O God, didst permit me to recover from that disease, and didst make the son of Thy handmaid whole, first in body, that he might become one on whom Thou couldst bestow a better and more secure restoration."

Again restored to health, he began to counsel his companions against Manichæism, to which before he had so zealously labored to win over adherents. And yet he could not lead them to the truth. His dislike to the Church had rather increased. The doctrine of the incarnation of the Son of God had become particularly offensive to him, as it was to all Gnostics and Manichæans. He despaired of finding truth in the Church. Yet scepticism could not satisfy him, and so he was tossed wildly between two waters, that would not flow peacefully together. "The more earnestly and perseveringly I reflected on the activity, the acuteness, and the depths of the human soul, the more I was led to believe that truth could not be a thing inaccessible to man, and came thus to the conclusion that the right path to its attainment had not hitherto been discovered, and that this path must be marked out by divine authority. But now the question arose what this divine authority might be, since among so many conflicting sects each professed to teach in its name. A forest full of mazes stood again before my eyes, in which I was to wander about, and to be compelled to tread, which rendered me fearful."

In this unsettled state of mind he felt himself drawn toward the doctrines of the New Academy.* This system, whose representatives were Arcesilaus and Carneades, denied, in most decided opposition to Stoicism, the possibility of an infallible knowledge of any object; it could only arrive at a subjective probability, not truth.

---

* *Confess.* V. 10 : "*Etenim suborta est etiam mihi cogitatio, prudentiores cœteris fuisse illos philosophos, quos Academicos appellant, quod de omnibus dubitandum esse censuerant, nec aliquid veri ab homine comprehendi posse decreverant.*"

But our church-father could not rest content with a philosophy so sceptical. It only served to give him a deeper sense of his emptiness, and thus, in a negative manner, to pave the way for something better. A change in his external circumstances soon occurred which hastened the great crisis of his life.

After he had been in Rome not quite a year the prefect Symmachus, the eloquent advocate of declining heathenism, was requested to send an able teacher of rhetoric to Milan. The choice fell on Augustin. The recommendation of Manichæan patrons, and still more his trial-speech, obtained for him the honorable and lucrative post. He forsook Rome the more willingly because the manners of the students did not please him. They were accustomed to leave one teacher in the midst of his course, without paying their dues, and go to another.

With this removal to Milan we approach the great crisis in the life of Augustin, when he was freed forever from the fetters of Manichæism and scepticism, and became a glorious light in the Church of Jesus Christ.

CHAPTER IX.

AUGUSTIN IN MILAN—ST. AMBROSE.

In the spring of the year 384 Augustin, accompanied by his old friend Alypius, journeyed to Milan, the second capital of Italy and frequent residence of the Roman Emperor.

The episcopal chair at that place was then filled by one

of the most venerable of the Latin fathers, one who not only earned enduring honors in the sphere of theology, but also in that of sacred poetry and sacred music, and distinguished himself as an ecclesiastical prince by the energetic and wise management of his diocese and his bold defence of the interests of the Church, even against the Emperor himself.

Ambrose was born at Treves, in the year 340, of a very ancient and illustrious family. His father was governor of Gaul, one of the three great dioceses of the Western Roman Empire. When yet a little boy, as he lay sleeping in the cradle with his mouth open, a swarm of bees came buzzing around, and flew in and out of his mouth, without doing him any harm. The father, astonished at the unexpected vanishing of the danger, cried out in a prophetic mood : "Truly, this child, if he lives, will turn out something great!" A similar story is told of Plato. After the early death of the prefect his pious widow moved to Rome with her three children, and gave them a careful education.

Ambrose was marked out for a brilliant worldly career by man, but not by God. After the completion of his studies he made his appearance as an attorney, and acquitted himself so well by his eloquent discourses that Probus, the governor of Italy, appointed him his counsellor. Soon after he conveyed to him the prefecture or viceregency of the provinces of Liguria and Æmilia, in Upper Italy, with the remarkable words, afterward interpreted as an involuntary prophecy : "Go, and act, not as judge, but as bishop." Ambrose administered his office with dignity, justice, and clemency, and won for himself universal esteem.

The Church of Milan was then involved in a battle between Arianism, which denied the divinity of Christ, and Nicene orthodoxy, which maintained the essential equality of the Son with the Father. Auxentius, an Arian, had succeeded in driving into exile the Catholic bishop Dionysius, and usurping the episcopal chair. But he died in the year 374.

At the election of a new bishop bloody scenes were apprehended. Ambrose thought it his duty as governor to go into the church and silence the uproar of the parties. His speech to the assembled multitude was suddenly interrupted by the cry of a child—"Ambrose, be bishop!" As swift as lightning the voice of the child became the voice of the people, who with one accord would have him and no other for their chief shepherd.

Ambrose was confounded. He was then still in the class of catechumens, and hence not baptized, and had, moreover, so high an opinion of the dignity and responsibility of the episcopal office that he deemed himself altogether unworthy of it and unfit for it. He resorted to flight, cunning, and the strangest devices to evade the call. But it availed nothing; and when now also the imperial confirmation of the choice arrived, he submitted to the will of God, which addressed him so powerfully through these circumstances. After being baptized by an orthodox bishop, and having run through the different clerical stages, he received episcopal consecration on the eighth day.

His friend Basil, of Cæsarea, was highly rejoiced at the result. "We praise God," so he wrote, "that in all ages He chooses such as are pleasing to Him. He once chose a shepherd and set him up as ruler over His people. Moses, as he tended the goats, was filled with the Spirit of God, and raised to the dignity of a prophet. But in our days He sent out of the royal city, the metropolis of the world, a man of lofty spirit, distinguished by noble birth and the splendor of riches and by an eloquence, at which the world wonders ; one who renounces all these earthly glories, and esteems them but loss that he may win Christ, and accepts, on behalf of the Church, the helm of a great ship made famous by his faith. So be of good cheer, O man of God !"

From this time forward until the day of his death, which occurred on Good Friday of the year 397, Ambrose acted the part of a genuine bishop : he was the shepherd of the congregation, the defender of the oppressed, the watchman of the Church, the teacher of the people, the adviser and reprover of kings. He began by distributing his lands, his gold, and his silver among the poor. His life was exceedingly severe and simple. He took no dinner, except on Saturdays, Sundays, and the festivals of celebrated martyrs. Invitations to banquets he declined, except when his office required his presence, and then he set an example of temperance. The day was devoted to the duties of his calling, the most of the night to prayer, meditation on divine things, the study of the Bible and the Greek fathers, and the writing of theological works. He preached every Sunday, and in cases of necessity during the week, sometimes twice a day. To his catechumens he attended with especial care, but exerted an influence on a wider circle by means of his writings, in which old Roman vigor, dignity, and sententiousness were united with a deep and ardent practical Christianity. He was easy of access to all—to the lowest as well as the highest. His revenues were given to the needy, whom he called, on this account, his stewards and treasurers. With dauntless heart he battled against the Arian heresy, and, as the Athanasius of the West, helped Nicene orthodoxy to its triumph in Upper Italy.

Such was Ambrose. If any one was fitted for winning over to the Church the highly-gifted stranger who came into his neighborhood, it was he. Augustin visited the bishop, not as a Christian, but as a celebrated and eminent man. He was received by him with paternal kindness, and at once felt himself drawn toward him in love. "Unconsciously was I led to him, my God, by Thee, in order to be consciously led by him to Thee." He also frequently attended his preaching, not that he might be converted by him, and obtain food for his soul, but that he might listen to a beautiful and eloquent sermon. The personal character and renown of Ambrose attracted him. The influence of curiosity was predominant; and yet it could not but happen that the contents of the discourses also should soon make an impression on him, even against his will.

"I began to love him," says he, "not, indeed, at first as a teacher of the truth, which I despaired of finding in Thy Church, but as a man worthy of my love. I often listened to his public discourses, I confess, not with a pure motive, but only to prove if his eloquence was equal to his fame. I weighed his words carefully, while I had no interest in their meaning, or despised it. I was delighted with the grace of his language, which was more learned, more full of intrinsic value, but in delivery less brilliant and flattering, than that of Faustus, the Manichæan. In regard to the contents, there was no comparison between them; for while the latter conducted into Manichæan errors, the former taught salvation in the surest way. From sinners, like I was then, salvation is indeed far off; yet was I gradually and unconsciously drawing near to it. For although it was not my wish to learn *what* he said, but only to hear *how* he said it (this vain interest was left me, who despaired of the truth), still, along with the words, which I loved, there stole also into my spirit the substance, which I had no care for, because I could not separate the two. And while I opened my heart to receive the eloquence which he uttered, the truth also which he spake found entrance, though by slow degrees."*

By this preaching the Old Testament was filled with new light to Augustin. He had imbibed a prejudice against it from the Manichæans. He regarded it as little else than a letter that kills. Ambrose unfolded its life-giving spirit by means of allegorical interpretation, which was then in vogue among the Fathers, especially those of the Alexandrian school. Its aim was, above all, to spiritualize the historical parts of the Bible, and to resolve the external husk into universal ideas. Thus gross violence was often done to the text, and things were dragged into the Bible, which, to an unbiassed mind, were not contained there, at least not in the exact place indicated. And yet this mode of interpretation was born of the spirit of faith and reverence, which bowed to the Word of God as to a source of the most profound truths, and, so far, was instructive and edifying. To Augustin, who himself used it freely in his writings, often to capriciousness, although he afterward inclined rather to a cautious, grammatical, and historical apprehension of the Scripture, it was then very acceptable, and had the good effect of weaning him still further from Manichæism. He soon threw it aside altogether. But even the Platonic philosophers, whom he preferred to it, he would not blindly trust, because "the saving name of Christ was wanting in them," from which, according to that ineffaceable impression of his pious childhood, he could never separate the knowledge of the truth.

* *Confess.* V. 13, 14.

CHAPTER X.

AUGUSTIN A CATECHUMEN IN THE CATHOLIC CHURCH.

We would suppose that he was now ready to cast himself into the arms of the Church, which approached him by a representative so worthy and so highly gifted. But he had not yet come so far. Various difficulties stood in the way. To think of God as a purely spiritual substance gave him peculiar trouble. In this he was yet under the influence of Manichæism, which clothed the spiritual idea of God in the garb of sense.

Nevertheless, he took a considerable step in advance. He enrolled himself in the class of the catechumens, to which he had already belonged when a boy, and resolved to remain there until he could arrive at a decision in his own soul.* He says of his condition at this time, that he had come so far already that any capable teacher would have found in him a most devoted and teachable scholar.

Thus did Augustin resign himself to the maternal care of the communion in which he had received his early, never-forgotten religious impressions. It could not happen otherwise than, after an honest search, he should at last discover in her the supernatural glory, which, to the offence of the carnal understanding, was concealed under the form of a servant. A man possessed of his ardent longing after God, his tormenting thirst for truth and peace of mind, could obtain rest only in the asylum

---

* *Confess.* V. 14 : " *Statui ergo tamdiu esse catechumenus in catholica ecclesia, mihi a parentibus commendata, donec aliquid certi eluceret, quo cursum dirigerem.*"

founded by God Himself, and see there all his desires fulfilled beyond his highest hopes.

The Church had then emerged from the bloody field of those witnesses who had joyfully offered up their lives to show their gratitude and fidelity to the Lord who had died for them. Their heroic courage, which overcame the world; their love, which was stronger than death; their patience, which endured cruel tortures without a murmur, as lambs led to the slaughter; and their hope, which burst out in songs of triumph at the stake and on the cross, were yet fresh in her memory. Everywhere altars and chapels were erected to perpetuate their virtues. From a feeling of thankfulness for the victory, so dearly purchased by their death, and in the consciousness of an uninterrupted communion with the glorified warriors, their heavenly birthdays were celebrated.* While heathenism, in the pride of its power, its literature, and its art, was falling into decay, the youthful Church, sure of her promise of eternal duration, pressed triumphantly forward into a new era, to take possession of the wild hordes of the invading nations who destroyed the Roman Empire, and communicate to them, along with faith in the Redeemer, civilization, morality, and the higher blessings of life. The most noble and profound spirits sought refuge in her communion, in which alone they could find rest for their souls and quench their thirst after truth. She fearlessly withstood the princes and potentates of earth, and reminded them of righteousness and judgment. In that stormy and despotic period she afforded shelter to the oppressed, was a kind and loving mother to the poor, the widow, and the orphan, and opened her treasures to all who needed help. They who

---

* So were the days of their death called.

were weary of life found in the peaceful cells of her monasteries, in communion with pilgrims of like spirit, an undisturbed retreat, where they could give themselves wholly up to meditation on divine things. Thus she cared for all classes, and brought consolation and comfort into every sphere of life. She zealously persevered in preaching and exhorting, in the education of youth for a better world, in prayer and in intercession for the bitterest enemies, and in ascriptions of glory to the Holy Trinity.

Her devotion concentrated itself on the festivals, recurring yearly in honor of the great facts of the Gospel, especially on Easter and Whitsuntide, when multitudes of catechumens, of both sexes and all ages, clad in white garments, the symbol of purity, were received into the ranks of Christ's warriors, amid fervent prayers and animating hymns of praise. The prince bowed with the peasant in baptism before the common Lord ; the famous scholar sat like a child among the catechumens ; and blooming virgins, "those lilies of Christ," as Ambrose calls them, made their vow before the altar to renounce the world and live for the heavenly bridegroom. The activity of Ambrose was in this respect attended by the richest results. He would frequently, on the solemn night before Easter, have as many incorporated into the communion of the Church by baptism as five other bishops together.

The Church of that time was still an undivided unity, without excluding, however, great diversity of gifts and powers. And this enabled her to overcome so victoriously heresies, schisms, persecutions, and the collected might of heathenism itself. One body and one spirit, one Lord, one faith, one baptism, one God and Father of all—this declaration of the apostle was more applicable to the first centuries of the Church than to later periods. The dweller on the Rhine found on the borders of the African desert, and the Syrian on the shores of the Rhone, the same confession of faith, the same sanctifying power, and the same ritual of worship. The Christian of the fourth century felt himself in living communion with all the mighty dead, who had long before departed in the service of the same Lord. That age had no idea of an interruption in the history of God's kingdom, a sinking away of the life-stream of Christ. From the heart of God and His Son it has rolled down, from the days of the apostles, through the veins of the Church Catholic, amid certain infallible signs, in one unbroken current to the present, in order gradually to fertilize the whole round of earth, and empty itself into the ocean of eternity.

And yet we have just as little reason to think the Church at that time free from faults and imperfections as at any other period. Some dream, indeed, of a golden age of spotless purity. But such an age has never been, and will only first appear after the general resurrection. Even the Apostolic Church was, in regard to its membership, by no means absolutely pure and holy; for we need only read attentively and with unbiassed mind any Epistle of the New Testament or the letters to the seven churches in the Apocalypse, in order to be convinced that they collectively reproved the congregations to which they were sent, for various faults, excrescences, and perversions, and warned them of manifold errors, dangers, and temptations. When, moreover, through the conversion of Constantine, the great mass of the heathen world crowded into the Church, they dragged along with them also a vast amount of corruption. A very sad and dreary picture of the Christianity of the Nicene period can be drawn from the writings of the fathers of the fourth century (Gregory Nazianzen, for example), so that the modern Church in comparison appears in many respects like a great improvement. The march of Christianity is steadily onward.

In spite of all these defects there were yet remedies and salt enough to preserve the body from decay. The militant Church, in her continuous conflict with a sinful world, must ever authenticate and develop the power of genuine sanctity, and this she did during the Nicene period. We cannot mistake the agency of the Holy Spirit, who, amid the stormy and passionate battles with Arianism and semi-Arianism, at last helped the Nicene faith to victory. And we cannot refuse genuine admiration to those great heroes of the fourth century, an Athanasius, a Basil, a Gregory of Nyssa, a Gregory of Nazianzum, a Chrysostom, an Ambrose, a Jerome, who were distinguished as much by earnestness and dignity of character and depth and vigor of piety as by their eminent learning and culture, and who are, even to this day, gratefully honored by the Greek, the Roman, and the Protestant communions as true church-*fathers*. Notwithstanding all the corruption in her bosom, the Catholic Church of that age was still immeasurably elevated above heathenism, sinking into hopeless ruin, and the conceited and arrogant schools of the Gnostics and Manichæans; for she, and she alone, was the bearer of the divine-human life-powers of the Christian religion, and the hope of the world.

CHAPTER XI.

ARRIVAL OF MONNICA.

Such was the state of the Church when Augustin entered the class of catechumens and listened attentively to her doctrines. His good genius, Monnica, soon came to Milan, as one sent by God. She could no longer stay in Africa without her son, and embarked for Italy. While at sea a storm arose, which made the oldest sailors tremble. But she, feeling strong and secure under the protection of the Almighty, encouraged them all, and confidently predicted a happy termination to the voyage; for God had promised it to her in a vision. In Milan she found her son delivered from the snares of Manichæism, but not yet a believing professor. She was highly rejoiced, and accepted the partial answer of her tearful prayers as a pledge of their speedy and complete fulfilment. "My son," said she, with strong assurance, "I believe in Christ, that before I depart this life I shall see thee become a believing, Catholic Christian." *

She found favor with Ambrose, who often spoke of her with great respect, and thought the son happy who had such a mother. She regularly attended his ministrations, and willingly gave up certain usages, which, though observed by her at home, were not in vogue at Milan, such as fasting on Saturdays and love-feasts at the graves of the martyrs. With renewed fervor and confi-

---

* *Confess.* VI. 1: " *Placidissime et pectore pleno fiduciæ respondit mihi, credere se in Christo, quod priusquam de hac vita emigraret me visura esset fidelem catholicum.*"

dence she now prayed to God, who had already led the darling of her heart to the gates of the sanctuary. She was soon to witness the fulfilment of her desires.

CHAPTER XII.

MORAL CONFLICTS—PROJECT OF MARRIAGE.

AUGUSTIN continued to listen to the discourses of Ambrose and visit him at his house, although the bishop, on account of pressing duties, could not enter so fully as he wished into his questions and doubts. He now obtained a more just idea of the doctrines of the Scriptures and the Church than the perversions of the Manichæans had afforded him. He saw "that all the knots of cunning misrepresentation which these modern betrayers of the Divine Word had tied up could be unloosed, and that for so many years he had been assailing, not the real faith of the Church, but chimeras of a fleshly imagination." He now first began to prize and comprehend the Bible in some measure, while before it had been to him a disagreeable volume, sealed with seven seals; and such it ever is to all those who wilfully tear it loose from living Christianity, and drag it into the forum of the carnal understanding, "which perceives not the things of the Spirit of God," and thus factiously constitute themselves judges over it, instead of surrendering themselves to it in humble obedience.

Meanwhile he had many practical and theoretical struggles to pass through before reaching a final decision. About this time, in conjunction with his friends, among whom were Alypius, who had come with him to Milan, and Nebridius, who had lately left Africa, in order to live together with Augustin, "in the most ardent study of truth and wisdom," he resolved to form a philosophical union, and, in undisturbed retirement, with a community of goods, to devote himself exclusively to the pursuit of truth. In such a self-created ideal world, which commended itself to the lofty imagination of one so gifted and noble as Augustin was, he sought a substitute for the reality of Christianity and the deeper earnestness of practical life and activity. "Diverse thoughts were thus in our hearts, but Thy counsel, O God, abides in eternity. According to that counsel Thou didst laugh at ours, and work out Thine own, to bestow on us the Spirit at the set time." "While the winds were blowing from every quarter and tossing my heart to and fro, time went by, and I delayed in turning to the Lord, and put off living in Thee from day to day, and did not put off dying daily in myself. Desiring a life of blessedness, I shunned the place where it dwelt, and sought it by flying from it."*

The romantic scheme fell to pieces, because the friends could not agree as to whether marriage ought to be wholly forbidden in their philosophical hermitage, as Alypius desired, in the fashion of the ascetic piety of that age, or not, as Augustin proposed. He was unable then to give up the love of women. "I believed I would become very unhappy if I was deprived of the embraces of woman, and I did not consider the medicine of Thy grace for the healing of this weakness, for I was inexperienced; for I esteemed continency an affair of natural ability of which I was not conscious, and was foolishly

---

* *Confess.* VI. 11 : " *Amando beatam vitam, timebam illam in sede sua, et ab ea fugiens quærebam eam.*"

ignorant of what the Scripture says (Wisdom viii. 21), that no one can be continent unless God gives him power. Surely, Thou wouldst have given it to me had I prayed to Thee with inward groaning, and with firm faith cast my care upon Thee!" *

On this account Augustin resolved to enter into formal wedlock, though for certain reasons the resolution was never carried into effect.

His mother, who, in common with the whole Church of that era, regarded perfect abstinence as a higher grade of virtue, still, under the circumstances, eagerly laid hold of the plan. In the haven of marriage she believed him secure from debauchery, and then every hindrance to his baptism, which she so ardently desired, was also taken away.

Both looked around for a suitable match. The choice was not easily made, for Augustin wished to find beauty, amiability, refinement, and some wealth united in one person. In this matter the mother, as usual, took counsel of God in prayer. At last a lady was discovered answerable to their wishes, who also gave her consent, but because of her youth the nuptials had to be postponed for two years longer.

Augustin immediately discharged his mistress, whom he had brought with him from Carthage, and who, as one would think, was best entitled to the offer of his hand. This conduct is a serious blot on his character, according to our modern notions of morality. But neither he nor Monnica looked upon it in that light, and were unconscious of doing any wrong. The unhappy outcast, who appears to have loved him truly, and had been faithful to him, as he to her, during the thirteen years of

---

* *Confess.* VI. 11.

their intercourse, returned to Africa with a heavy heart, and vowed that she would never know any other man. Their natural son, Adeodatus, she left with his father.

Just after the separation Augustin felt with bleeding heart the strength of his unlawful attachment. So strong had the power of sensuality become in him through habit, that neither the recollections of the departed nor respect for his bride could restrain him from forming a new immoral connection for the interval. Along with this carnal lust came also the seductions of ambition and a longing after a brilliant career in the world. He felt very miserable ; he must have been ashamed before his own better self, before God and man. "But the more miserable I felt, the nearer didst Thou come to me, O God." The Disposer of his life had His hand over all this. "I thought, and Thou wert with me ; I sighed, and Thou heardst me ; I was tossed about, yet Thou didst pilot me ; I wandered on the broad way, and still Thou didst not reject me."

CHAPTER XIII.

MENTAL CONFLICTS.

YET more violent and painful were his theoretical conflicts, the tormenting doubts of his philosophic spirit.

The question concerning the origin of evil, which once attracted him to the Manichæans, was again brooded over with renewed interest. The heresy that evil is a substance, and co-eternal with God, he had rejected. But whence then was it ? The Church found its origin in the will of the creature, who was in the beginning good, and of his own free choice estranged himself from God. But here the question arose, Is not the possibility of evil, imprinted by God in its creation on the will, itself already the germ of evil? Or could not God, as the Almighty, have so created the will as to render the fall impossible? How can He then be a Being of perfect goodness? And if we transfer the origin of evil, as the Church does, from the human race to Satan, through whose temptation Adam fell, the difficulty is not thereby settled, but only pushed further back. Whence, then, the Devil? and if he was first transformed from a good angel into a devil by a wicked will, whence then that wicked will?

Here he was again met by the spectre of Gnostic and Manichæan dualism, but soon reverted to the idea of the absolute God, whom he had made the immovable ground-pillar of his thinking, and who naturally cannot suffer the admission of a second absolute existence. Perhaps evil is a mere shadow. But how can anything unreal and empty prepare such fears and torments for the conscience?

He revolved such questions in his mind, and found no peace. "Thou, my God—Thou alone knowest what I suffered, but no one among men." He was not able to communicate fully the tumult of his soul even to his most intimate friends. But these conflicts had the good effect of driving him to prayer and strengthening in him the conviction that mind, left to itself, can never reach a satisfactory result.

CHAPTER XIV.

INFLUENCE OF PLATONISM.

ABOUT this time, somewhere in the beginning of the year 386, he fell in with certain Platonic and New Platonic writings, translated into Latin by the rhetorician Victorinus, who afterward was converted to Christianity. No doubt he had a general acquaintance with this philosophy before. But now, for the first time, he studied it earnestly in its original sources, to which he was introduced by an admiring disciple. He himself says that it kindled in him an incredible ardor.*

Platonism is beyond dispute the noblest product of heathen speculation, and stands in closer contact with Revelation than any other philosophical system of antiquity. It is in some measure an unconscious prophecy of Christ, in whom alone its sublime ideals can ever become truth and reality. The Platonic philosophy is distinguished by a lofty ideality, which raises man above the materialistic doings and sensual views of every-day life into the invisible world, to the contemplation of truth, beauty, and virtue. It is genuine *philosophy*, or love of wisdom, home-sickness—deep longing and earnest search after truth. It reminds man of his original likeness to God, and thus gives him a glimpse of the true end of all his endeavor.

Platonism also approaches Revelation in several of its

---

* *Contr. Academ.* II. 5 : " *E iam mihi ipsi de me ipso incredibile incendium in me concitarunt.*" Comp. my *History of the Apost. Church.* p. 150 sqq., and my *Church History*, vol. II. p. 95 sqq., where the relation of Platonism to Christianity and to the Church Fathers is discussed in detail.

doctrines, at least in the form of obscure intimation. We may here mention its presentiment of the unity, and, in a certain measure, the trinity of the Divine Being; the conception that the world of ideas is alone true and eternal, and the world of sense its copy; and further, that the human soul has fallen away from a condition of original purity, and merited its present suffering existence in the prison of the body; but that it should have longing aspirations after its home, the higher world, free itself from the bonds of sense, and strive after the highest spiritual and eternal good.

Hence it was no wonder that Platonism to many cultivated heathens and some of the most prominent fathers, especially in the Greek Church, became a theoretical schoolmaster for leading to Christ, as the Law was a practical schoolmaster to the Jews. It delivered Augustin completely from the bondage of Manichæan dualism and Academic scepticism, and turned his gaze inward and upward. In the height of his enthusiasm he believed that he had already discovered the hidden fountain of wisdom. But he had soon to learn that not the abstract knowledge of the truth, but living in it, could alone give peace to the soul; and that this end could only be reached in the way of divine revelation and practical experience of the heart.

Although the Platonic philosophy contained so many elements allied to Christianity, there were yet two important points not found therein: first, the great mystery, the Word made flesh; and then love, resting on the basis of humility.* The Platonic philosophy held up before him beautiful ideals, without giving him power

---

* *Confess.* VII. 20: "*Ubi enim erat illa caritas ædificans a fundamento humilitatis, quod est Christus Jesus? Aut quando illi libri* [*Platonici*] *docerent me eam?*"

to attain them. If he attempted to seize them ungodly impulses would suddenly drag him down again into the mire.

CHAPTER XV.

STUDY OF THE SCRIPTURES.

Thus the admonition to study the Holy Scriptures was addressed to him once more, and in a stronger tone than ever. He now gave earnest heed to it, and drew near the holy volume with deep reverence and a sincere desire for salvation.*

He was principally carried away with the study of the Epistles of St. Paul, and read them through collectively with the greatest care and admiration. Here he found all those truths which addressed him in Platonism no longer obscurely foreshadowed, but fulfilled; and yet much more besides. Here he found Christ as the Mediator between God and man, between heaven and earth, who alone can give us power to attain those lofty ideals and embody them in life. Here he read that masterly delineation of the conflict between the spirit and the flesh (Rom. vii.), which was literally confirmed by his own experience. Here he learned to know aright the depth of the ruin and the utter impossibility of being delivered from it by any natural wisdom or natural strength, and, at the same time, the great remedy which God graciously offers to us in His beloved Son.

Such light, such consolation, and such power the Pla-

---

* *Confess.* VII. 21: " *Itaque avidissime arripui venerabilem stilum Spiritus tui, et præ cæteris Apostolum Paulum,*" etc.

tonic writings had never yielded. "On their pages," he says very beautifully, in the close of the seventh book of his *Confessions*, "no traces of piety like this can be discovered; tears of penitence; Thy sacrifice, the broken spirit; the humble and the contrite heart; the healing of the nations; the Bride, the City of God; the earnest of the Holy Spirit; the cup of our salvation. No one sings there: 'Truly my soul waiteth upon God; from Him cometh my salvation; He only is my rock and my salvation; He is my high tower; I shall not be greatly moved.' (Ps. lxii. 1, 2.) There no one hears the invitation: 'Come unto me, all ye that labor and are heavy-laden, and I will give you rest.' (Matt. xi. 28.) They [the Platonists] disdain to learn of Him who is meek and lowly in heart; they cannot imagine why the lowly should teach the lowly, nor understand what is meant by His taking the form of a servant. For Thou hast hidden it from the wise and prudent, and revealed it unto babes. It is one thing to see afar off, from the summit of a woody mountain, the fatherland of peace, and without any path leading thither, to wander around lost and weary among byways, haunted by lions and dragons, that lurk in ambush for their prey; and quite another to keep safely on a road that leads thither, guarded by the care of a Celestial Captain, where no robbers, who have forsaken the heavenly army, ever lie in wait. This made a wonderful impression on my spirit, when I read the humblest of Thine Apostles (1 Cor. xv. 9), and considered Thy works, and saw the depths of sin."

CHAPTER XVI.

AUGUSTIN'S CONVERSION.

We now stand on the threshold of his conversion. Theoretically he was convinced of the truth of the doctrines of the Church, but practically had yet to undergo, in his bitter experience, the judgment of St. Paul: "The flesh lusteth against the spirit, and the spirit against the flesh." (Gal. v. 17.) No sooner did his soul rise into the pure ether of communion with God than the cords of sense drew him down again into the foul atmosphere of earth. "The world," said he, "lost its charms before Thy sweetness and before the glory of Thy house, which I had learned to love; but I was yet bound by strong ties to a woman." "I had found the beautiful pearl; I should have sold all I possessed to buy it, and yet I hesitated."

Amid the tumult of the world he often sighed after solitude. Desiring counsel, and unwilling to disturb the indefatigable Ambrose, he betook himself to the venerable priest Simplicianus, who had grown gray in the service of his Master. The priest described to him, for his encouragement, the conversion of his friend Victorinus, a learned teacher of rhetoric at Rome, and translator of the Platonic writings, who had passed over from the Platonic philosophy to a zealous study of the Scriptures, and cordially embraced the Saviour with a sacrifice of great worldly gain. For a long time he believed he could be a Christian without joining the Church, and when Simplicianus replied to him: "I will not count you a Christian before I see you in the Church of Christ," Victorinus asked with a smile: "Do the walls, then, make Christians?" * But afterward he came to see that he who does not confess Christ openly before the world need not hope to be confessed by Him before His Heavenly Father (Matt. x. 32, 33), and therefore submitted in humble faith to the washing of baptism.

Augustin wished to do likewise, but his will was not yet strong enough. He compares his condition to that of a man drunk with sleep, who wishes to rise up, but now for the first time rightly feels the sweetness of slumber, and sinks back again into its arms. In a still more warning and pressing tone the voice sounded in his ears: "Awake, thou that sleepest, and arise from the dead, and Christ shall shine upon thee" (Eph. v. 14); but he answered lazily: "Soon, yes, soon! only wait a little;" and the *soon* passed on into hours, days, and weeks. In vain his inward man delighted in the law of God, for another law in his members warred against the law of his mind, and brought him into captivity to the law of sin. (Rom. vii. 22, 23.) His disquietude rose higher and higher; his longing became violent agony. Oftentimes he would tear his hair, smite his forehead, wring his hands about his knees, and cry out despairingly: "O wretched man that I am! who shall deliver me out of the body of this death?" (Rom. vii. 24.)

These conflicts, in connection with the weight of his literary labors, had exerted such an injurious influence on his health that he began to think seriously of resigning his post as a rhetorician.

One day, as he sat in a downcast mood with his bosom friend Alypius, who was involved in similar struggles,

---

* *Confess.* VIII. 2: "*Ergo parietes faciunt Christianos?*" This passage is sometimes torn from its connection and misused for a purpose directly opposite; since Augustin quotes it to show that a man could not be a Christian without joining the visible Church.

their countryman Pontitianus, a superior officer in the Roman army, and at the same time a zealous Christian, entered the chamber. He was surprised, instead of a classic author or a Manichæan writer, to see the Epistles of Paul lying on the table. He began a religious conversation, and in the course of his remarks took occasion to speak of the Egyptian hermit Anthony (died 356), who, in literal pursuance of the Saviour's advice to the rich young man (Matt. xix. 21), had given up all his property in order to live to the Lord unrestricted and undisturbed, in solitude, and there to work out the salvation of his soul. The two friends had as yet heard nothing of the wonderful saint of the desert, the venerable father of monachism, and just as little of a cloister outside of the walls of Milan, under the supervision of Ambrose, and were now charmed and ashamed at the information. Their countryman related further how, during his stay at Treves, two of his friends, who were both engaged to be married, obtained, on a visit to a cell, the biography of Anthony ascribed to Athanasius, the great "father of orthodoxy," and on reading it fell so in love with the contemplative life and the higher perfection there portrayed, that they threw up their commissions in the army and took leave of the world forever. Their brides did likewise.

This was a sting for the conscience of Augustin. The soldiers and their brides had heard the call of the Lord only once, and obeyed it immediately. And he? It was now more than twelve years since the *Hortensius* of Cicero had stirred him up so powerfully to search after truth, and ever clearer and clearer the voice of the Good Shepherd had sounded in his ears. And yet his will rose up in rebellion ; he was not ready to renounce the world *wholly*, but desired to retain at least some of its pleasures.

Pontitianus left the house. Then the storm in the soul of Augustin broke loose with greater violence, and expressed itself in the features of his countenance, his looks, and his gestures still more than in his words. " What has happened to us ?" said he to Alypius—" what is it ? What hast thou heard ? The unlearned rise up and lay hold of the kingdom of heaven, and we, with our heartless knowledge—see how we wallow in flesh and blood ! Shall we be ashamed to follow them because they have gone before, and not ashamed not to follow them at all ?" *

After he had said this, and more in a similar strain, he rushed out with the Epistles of Paul in his hand into an adjoining garden, where no one would be likely to interrupt the agitation of his soul until God Himself should allay it. For it was, as he said, despair or salvation, death or life. Alypius followed in his footsteps.

" We removed as far as possible from the house. I groaned in spirit, full of stormy indignation that I had not entered into covenant and union with Thee, my God, and all my bones cried out ; thither must thou go ! But it was not possible to go by ship, or wagon, or on foot, as we go to any place we please. For going thither and coming there is nothing else than to *will* to go thither, and to will with *full* power—not to waver and be tossed to and fro with a divided will, which now rises up and now sinks down in the struggle." † He was angry at the perverseness of his will : " The spirit orders the body, and it obeys instantly ; the spirit orders itself, and

---

* *Confess.* VIII. 8.

† *Confess.* VIII. 8 : " *Nam non solum ire, verum etiam pervenire illuc, nihil erat aliud, quam velle ire, sed velle fortiter et integre ; non semisaucium hac atque hac versare et jactare voluntatem, parte adsurgente cum alia parte cadente luctantem.*"

it refuses. The spirit orders the hand to move, and it does it so quickly that one can scarcely distinguish between the act and the command; the spirit commands the spirit to will, and although the same, it will not do it. Whence this monstrosity? It is a disease of the spirit that prevents it from rising up; the will is split and divided; thus there are two wills in conflict with each other, one good and one evil, and I myself it was who willed and who did not will."

Thus was he pulled hither and thither, accusing himself more severely than ever, and turning and rolling in his fetters until they should be wholly broken, by which, indeed, he was no longer *wholly* bound, but only *yet*.

And when he had thus dragged up all his misery from its mysterious depths, and gathered it before the eye of his soul, a huge storm arose that discharged itself in a flood of tears.*

In such a frame of mind he wished to be alone with his God, and withdrew from Alypius into a retired corner of the garden. Here Augustin, he knew not how, threw himself down upon the earth, under a fig-tree, and gave free vent to his tears. "Thou, my Lord," he cried, with sobbing voice, "how long yet? O Lord, how long yet wilt Thou be angry? Remember not the sins of my youth! How long? how long? To-morrow, and again, to-morrow? Why not to-day, why not now? Why not in this hour put an end to my shame?" †

---

* *Confess.* VIII. 12: "*Oborta est procella ingens, ferens ingentem imbrem lacrymarum.*"

† *Confess.* VIII. 12: "*Et non quidem his verbis, sed in hac sententia multa dixi tibi: Et tu Domine, usquequo? Usquequo, Domine, irasceris in finem? Ne memor fueris iniquitatum nostrarum antiquarum! Sentiebam enim eis me teneri. Jactabam voces miserabiles: Quamdiu? Quamdiu? Cras et cras? Quare non modo? Quare non hac hora finis turpitudinis meae? Dicebam haec, et flebam amarissima contritione cordis mei.*"

Thus he prayed, supplicated, sighed, wrestled, and wept bitterly. They were the birth-pangs of the new life. From afar he saw the Church in the beauty of holiness. The glorified spirits of the redeemed, who had been snatched from the abyss by the All-merciful and transplanted into a heavenly state of being, beckoned to him. Still more powerfully the longing burned within him; still more hot and rapidly beat the pulse of desire after the Saviour's embrace; as a weary, hunted stag after the fresh water-brooks, so panted his heart after the living God and a draught from the chalice of His grace.

The hour of deliverance had now come. The Lord had already stretched out His hand to tear asunder the last cords that bound his prodigal son to the world, and press him to a warm, true father's heart.

As Augustin was thus lying in the dust and ashes of repentance, and agonizing with his God in prayer, he suddenly heard from a neighboring house, as though from some celestial height, the sweet voice, whether of a boy or a maiden he knew not, calling out again and again, "*Tolle lege, tolle lege!*" *i.e.*, "Take and read." It was a voice from God that decided his heart and life. "Then I repressed," so he further relates in the last chapter of the eighth book of his *Confessions*, "the gush of tears, and raised myself up, while I received the word as nothing else than a divine injunction to open the Scriptures and read the first chapter that would catch my eye. I had heard how Anthony, once accidentally present during the reading of the gospel in church, had felt himself admonished, as though what was read had been specially aimed at him: 'Go, sell that thou hast, and give to the poor, and thou shalt have treasure in heaven; and come, follow me' (Matt. xix. 20), and that, by this oracle, he had been immediately converted, my God, to Thee."

He hastened to the place where he had left the Holy Book, and where Alypius sat ; snatched it up, opened, and read : "LET US WALK HONESTLY, AS IN THE DAY ; NOT IN REVELLING AND DRUNKENNESS, NOT IN CHAMBERING AND WANTONNESS, NOT IN STRIFE AND JEALOUSY. BUT PUT YE ON THE LORD JESUS CHRIST, AND MAKE NOT PROVISION FOR THE FLESH, TO FULFIL THE LUSTS THEREOF." (Rom. xiii. 13, 14.)*

This passage of the Epistle to the Romans was exactly suited to his circumstances. It called on him to renounce his old, wild life, and begin a new life with Christ. He found still more in it, according to the ascetic spirit of the age, and resolved to renounce all the honors and pleasures of the world, even his contemplated marriage, in order to devote himself, without restraint, to the service of the Lord and His Church, and, if possible, to attain the highest grade of moral perfection.†

He read no further. That single word of God was

---

* After the original and the Vulgate : "*et carnis providentiam ne feceritis in concupiscentiis,*" which Augustin, in his present condition, understood as a challenge to renounce completely every desire of the flesh. Luther, on the contrary, has translated it : "*Wartet des Leibes, doch also, dass er nicht geil werde,*" which gives a different sense. But in such a case $\sigma\tilde{\omega}\mu\alpha$ would be used in the Greek instead of $\sigma\acute{\alpha}\rho\xi$, and the conjunctive particle $\mu\acute{\eta}$ would stand after and not before $\pi\rho\acute{o}\nu o\iota\alpha\nu$.

† *Confess.* VIII. 12: "*Convertisti me ad te, ut nec uxorem quaererem, nec aliquam spem sæculi hujus,*" etc. Anthony, whose example had wrought powerfully in the conversion of Augustin, had, likewise, in literal accordance with the words of Christ (Matt. xix. 21), sold all that he had, and given it to the poor. According to the views of the ancient Church, which can be traced back as far as the second century, voluntary poverty, celibacy, and martyrdom were the way to a more literal following of Christ and a higher grade of holiness and bliss.

sufficient to decide his whole future. The gloomy clouds of doubt and despondency rolled away; the forgiveness of his sins was sealed to him; peace and joy streamed into his bosom. With his finger on the passage read, he shut the book, and told Alypius what had happened. The latter wished to read the words, and hit upon the next following verse (xiv. 1), "Him that is weak in the faith receive ye." He applied the warning to himself.

Both hastened, in the first ardor of conversion, to Monnica. The faithful soul must hear the glad tidings before others. She cried aloud and exulted, and her heart overflowed with thankfulness to the Lord, who, at last, after long, long delay, had answered beyond her prayers and comprehension.

This occurred in September of the year 386, in the thirty-third year of his life. Truly says Augustin: "All who worship Thee must, when they hear this, cry out: Blessed be the Lord, in heaven and on earth; great and wonderful is His name!"

CHAPTER XVII.

SOJOURN IN THE COUNTRY.

AUGUSTIN continued in office the few remaining weeks, till the autumnal holidays, and then handed in his resignation as public teacher of forensic eloquence, partly on account of a weakness of the breast, but chiefly because he had firmly resolved to consecrate himself henceforth wholly and entirely to the pursuit of divine things.

Along with his mother, his son, and his brother Navigius, Alypius, and other friends, he now withdrew to Cassiciacum, a villa lying near Milan, which belonged to his friend Verecundus.* He passed six months there under the serene Italian sky, in view of the glorious Swiss Alps, devoted to quiet meditation and preparation for the rite of holy baptism.

He had asked the advice of Ambrose as to what parts of Scripture he ought to study under his peculiar circumstances. The bishop recommended the Prophecies of Isaiah. But as Augustin could not rightly understand them he selected the Psalms, and found there just what he desired—the hallowed expression of his deepest religious feelings, from the low, sad wail of penitence and contrition up to the inspiring song of praise to the Divine Mercy. Half the night he spent in their study and in pious meditation, and enjoyed most blessed hours of intimate communion with God. He now mourned over and pitied the Manichæans for being so blind in regard to the Old Testament, which they rejected. "I wished only," he once thought, "they could have been in my neighborhood without my knowing it, and could have seen my face and heard my voice when in that retirement I read the Fourth Psalm, and how that Psalm wrought upon me."

A great part of the day he devoted to the education of two young men from his native city. His propensity for speculative meditation was so strong that he resorted with his company, in good weather, to the shade of a large tree, and in bad to the halls of the baths belonging to the villa, and, walking up and down in the freest

---

* Probably near the town Casciago in Lombardy, at the foot of a group of hills, from which there is a sublime view of the Monte Rosa.

manner, delivered discourses on those philosophical subjects which stood in the nearest relation to the most weighty practical interests of the heart—such as the knowledge of the truth, the idea of genuine wisdom, the life of blessedness and the way to it. Monnica took part in the discussion, and showed a rare degree of good sense and strength of intellect, so that the men forgot her sex and thought that "some great man was in their circle." These discourses were written down, and thus the earliest works of the great theologian, mostly philosophical in their contents, took their rise.

Of these the most important are : First, three books against the sceptical school of the Later Academy (*Contra Academicos*), which denied the possibility of knowing the truth. In opposition it was shown that scepticism either abrogates itself or, in a modified form, as a scheme of probabilities, bears witness to the existence of truth, for the probable must presuppose the true. Not the mere striving after truth, only the possession of it, can render happy. But it is only to be found in God, since He alone is happy who is in God and God in Him. The second discourse is a tract on the Life of Blessedness (*De Beata Vita*), in which these latter thoughts are further developed. And last, his "Soliloquies," or Discourses with his own Soul, concerning God, concerning the highest good, concerning his own nature, immortality, and the like. From these we will quote a single passage, to show the state of his mind at that time.

"O God, Creator of the world"—thus he prayed to the Lord—"grant me, first of all, grace to call upon Thee in a manner well-pleasing unto Thee ; that I may so conduct myself, that Thou mayest hear and then help me. Thou God, through whom all, that cannot be of itself, rises into being ; who even dost not suffer to fall into destruction what would destroy itself ; who never workest evil and rulest over the power of evil ; who revealest unto the few who seek after a true existence that evil can be overcome ; God, to whom the universe, in spite of evil, is perfect ; God, whom what can love, loves consciously or unconsciously ; God, in whom all is, and whom yet neither the infamy of the creature can disgrace, nor his wickedness defile, nor his error lead astray ; God, who hast preserved the knowledge of the truth for the pure alone ; Father of truth, Father of wisdom, Father of true and perfect life, Father of blessedness, Father of the good and the beautiful, Father of our awakening and enlightening, Father of the promise by which we are encouraged to return unto Thee, I invoke Thee, O Truth, in which and from which and by which all is true, that is true ; O Wisdom, in which and from which and by which all is wise, that is wise ; O true and most perfect Life, in which and from which and by which all lives, that lives ; O Blessedness, in which and from which and by which all is blessed, that is blessed ; O Beauty and Goodness, in which and from which and by which all is good and beautiful, that is good and beautiful ; O spiritual Light, in which and from which and by which all is spiritually light, that is spiritually light ; God, from whom to turn away is to fall, to whom to turn again is to rise, in whom to remain is to endure ; God, from whom to withdraw is to die, to whom to return is to live again, in whom to dwell is to live ; O God, Thou who dost sanctify and prepare us for an everlasting inheritance, bow down Thyself to me in pity ! Come to my help, Thou one, eternal, true Essence, in whom there is no discord, no confusion, no change, no need, no death, but the highest unity, the highest purity, the highest durability, the highest fulness, the highest life. Hear, hear, hear me, my God, my Lord, my King, my Father, my Hope, my Desire, my Glory, my Habitation, my Home, my Salvation, my Light, my Life, hear, hear, hear me, as Thou art wont to hear Thy Chosen.

"Already, I love Thee alone, follow Thee alone, seek Thee alone, am prepared to serve Thee only, because Thou alone rulest in righteousness. O command and order what Thou wilt, but heal and open mine ears, that I may hear Thy word ; deal and open mine eyes, that I may see Thy nod ; drive out my delusion, that I may recognize Thee again. O gracious Father, take back again Thy wanderer. Have I not been chastised enough ? Have I not long enough served Thine enemies, whom Thou hast under Thy feet—long enough been the sport of deception ? Receive me as Thy servant, for I fly from those who received me as a stranger, when I fled from Thee. Increase in me faith, hope, love, according to Thy wonderful and inimitable goodness.

"I desire to come to Thee, and again implore Thee for that by which I may come. For where Thou forsakest, there is destruction; but Thou dost not forsake, because Thou art the Highest Good, which every one, who seeks aright, will surely find. But he seeks it aright, to whom Thou hast given power to seek aright. Grant me power, O Father, to seek Thee aright; shield me from error! Let me not, when I seek, find another in Thy stead. I desire none other but Thee; O let me yet find Thee, my Father! But such a desire is vain, since Thou Thyself canst purify me and fit me to behold Thee.

"Whatever else the welfare of my mortal body may need, I commit into Thy hands, most wise and gracious Father, as long as I do not know what may be good for me, or those whom I love, and will, therefore, pray just as Thou wilt make it known at the time. Only this I beseech out of Thy great mercy, that Thou wilt convert me wholly unto Thyself, and when I obtain Thee, suffer me to be nothing else, and grant also, that, as long as I live and bear about this body, I may be pure and magnanimous, just and wise, filled with love and the knowledge of Thy wisdom, and worthy of an entrance into Thy blessed kingdom."

There are few traces of a specific churchly character in these writings. They exhibit rather a Platonism full of high thoughts, ideal views, and subtle dialectics, informed and hallowed by the spirit of Christianity. Many things were retracted by him at a later period— *e.g.*, the Platonic opinion that the human soul had a preexistence before its present life, and that the learning of a science is a restoration of it to memory, a disinterment, so to speak, of knowledge already existing, but covered over in the mind. He had yet many steps to take before reaching the depth and clearness of Christian knowledge which distinguished his later writings, and before the new life obtained full mastery within.

After his conversion, he did indeed abandon unlawful sexual intercourse. But now the pictures of his former sensual indulgence not seldom troubled his fancy in dreams. This he regarded as sin, and reproached himself bitterly. "Am I," he cried out—"am I not then dreaming what I am, O Lord, my God? Is not Thy mighty hand able to purge all the weakness of my soul, and frighten away with more abundant grace the concupiscence of my dreams? Yea, Thou wilt grant unto me more and more Thy gifts, that my soul may follow Thee and be with Thee even in dreams full of purity; Thou, who art able to do more than we can ask or understand."

CHAPTER XVIII.

AUGUSTIN'S BAPTISM.

In the beginning of the year 387 he returned to Milan, and along with his preparation for baptism kept up his literary activity. He wished to portray the different steps of human knowledge by which he himself had been gradually led to absolute knowledge, for the purpose of leading others to the sanctuary, and wrote works on grammar, logic, rhetoric, geometry, arithmetic, philosophy, music, and on the immortality of the soul, of which only the last two were completed and have come down to us.*

Meanwhile the wished-for hour of baptism arrived. On Easter Sabbath of this year he received, at the hands of the venerable Ambrose, this holy sacrament, in company with his friend Alypius, who, as he says, always differed from him for the better, and with his son Adeodatus, who was now fifteen years of age, and, preserved

---

* The book on grammar and the principles of logic and rhetoric in the first volume of the Benedictine edition of Augustin's works is spurious, because it lacks the form of dialogue and the higher bearing which he gave to his writings on these subjects.

from the evil courses of his father, had surrendered to the Lord his youthful soul, with all its rare endowments.

This solemn act and the succeeding festivals of Easter and Whitsuntide, in which the Church entered her spiritual spring, and basked in the warm sunlight of a Saviour risen from the dead and eternally present by his Spirit, made the deepest impression upon Augustin.

The solemnity of this festival was still further heightened by two circumstances—one connected with superstition and relic-worship, the other with the effect of hymns upon the heart.

The first was the miraculous discovery of the long-concealed relics of the traditional protomartyrs of Milan, Protasius and Gervasius—two otherwise unknown Roman citizens and missionaries—who were believed to have been beheaded in the persecution of Nero or Domitian. These relics were conveyed into the Ambrosian Basilica, and, according to the current belief of that credulous age, wrought there an astonishing miracle in support of Nicene orthodoxy against the Arian heresy.*

---

* *Confess.* IX. 7 : " Then didst Thou, by a vision, discover to Thy forenamed bishop [Ambrose] where the bodies of Gervasius and Protasius, the martyrs, lay hid (whom Thou hadst in Thy secret treasury stored uncorrupted so many years), whence Thou mightest seasonably produce them to repress the fury of a woman, but an Empress [Justina]." Then Augustin relates the healing of demoniacs and of a blind man by the touch of the relics. He again refers to this noted miracle, in *De Civ. Dei* xxii. 8, as having occurred in the presence of an immense multitude. Ambrose explained it at length in a sermon, wherein he said that the Arians admitted the fact of healing, but denied the cause. Comp. his letter to his sister, Marcellina, *Ep.* xxii. (al. LIV.). These are the two authorities for the legend of the protomartyrs of Milan. The subject of post-apostolic miracles is involved in inextricable difficulties. Augustin himself is not consistent in this matter. See his opinions in Schaff's *Church History*, vol. iii., 459 sqq.

Just then, also, Ambrose had transplanted the Church-hymns of the East into his congregation, and had added to them, as the father of Latin hymnody, productions of his own, conceived and executed in a noble, liturgical style. "I could not," says Augustin, "satiate myself in those days with the wonderful delight of meditating on the depth of Thy divine counsel in the salvation of the human race. How did I weep amid Thy hymns and chants, powerfully moved by the sweetly-sounding voice of Thy Church! Those tones poured into my ear; the truth dropped into my heart, and kindled there the fire of devotion; tears ran down my cheeks in the fulness of my joy!"*

As is well known, Ambrose gets credit as the author of the magnificent anthem, *Te Deum laudamus*, which is worthy of a place among David's Psalms of thanksgiving. A mediæval tradition says that it was composed by Ambrose and Augustin jointly, during the baptism of the latter, as if by inspiration from above, each singing in response, verse after verse. But neither Ambrose nor Augustin alludes to it anywhere. The *Te Deum* is of much later date (the sixth century), though several lines can be traced to an older Greek original.

CHAPTER XIX.

MONNICA'S LAST DAYS AND DEATH.

Soon after his baptism, in the summer of the year 387, he entered on his homeward journey to Africa, in company with his relatives and friends, in order to con-

---

* *Confess.* IX. 6.

tinue there the life of divine contemplation already begun in Cassiciacum. Among them was Evodius of Tagaste, a cultivated man, who was baptized a short time before, and now forsook the service of the Emperor to live in like manner exclusively for the higher world.

Already had they reached Ostia at the mouth of the Tiber, about a day's journey from Rome; already had they made the necessary preparations for embarking, when the sudden death of Monnica frustrated the plan. The faithful soul had now experienced the highest joy for which she had wished to live—she had seen the Saviour in the heart of her son, and could, like Hannah and Simeon of old, depart in peace to that true home which is more beautiful and sweeter far than Africa.

One day Augustin sat with his mother at a garden-window in Ostia, and conversed with her about the rest of eternity and its holy pleasures, which no eye has seen and no ear heard, but which God has prepared for them that love Him. Let us listen to his own narrative:

"Forgetting the past, and looking only toward the future, we asked ourselves, in the presence of the Truth, which Thou art, what the eternal life of the saints will be. And we opened longingly the mouths of our hearts to receive the celestial overflowings of Thy fountain, the fountain of life, that is with Thee, that being bedewed from it according to our capacity, we might meditate carefully upon this solemn subject. When now our discourse had reached that point, that no pleasure of corporeal sense, regarded in what brilliant light soever, durst for a moment be named with the glory of that life, much less compared with it, we mounted upward in ardent longing, and wandered step by step through all the material universe—the heavens, from which sun, moon, and stars beam down upon the earth. And we rose yet higher in inward thought, discourse, and admiration of Thy wonderful works, and on the wings of the spirit we rose above these also, in order to reach yon sphere of inexhaustible fulness, where Thou dost feed Israel to all eternity upon the pastures of Truth, where life is, and Truth by which all was made, that was there and will be. But truth itself was not made; it is as it was and always will be; for *to have been* and *to be* are not in it, but *being*, because it is eternal. For to *have been* and *to be* are not eternal. While we were thus talking and desiring, we touched it gently in full rapture of heart, and left bound there the first-fruits of the Spirit, and turned again to the sound of our lips, where the word begins and ends. And what is like Thy Word, our Lord, who remains unchanged in Himself, and renews all? We spake thus: If the tumult of the flesh were silent, and the images of earth, sea, and air were silent, and the poles were silent, and the soul itself were silent, transcending its own thoughts; if dreams and the revelations of fancy, and every language, and every sign, and everything represented by them were silent; if all were silent, for to him who hears, all these say, we have not made ourselves, but He who made us dwells in eternity; if, at this call, they were now silent, with ear uplifted to their Creator, and He should speak alone, not by them, but unmediated, so that we heard *His own Word*, not through a tongue of flesh, not through the voice of an angel, not through the roar of thunder, not through the dark outlines of a similitude, but from Himself, whom we love in them, and whom, without them, we heard as we now mounted, and with the rapid flight of thought touched the eternal truth that lies beyond them all; if this contemplation should continue, and no other foreign visions mingle with it, and if this alone should take hold of, and absorb, and wrap up its beholder in more inward joys, and such a life as that of which, now recovering our breath, we have had a momentary taste, were to last forever, would not then the saying, 'Enter into the joy of your Lord,' be fulfilled ?"

In the presentiment that she would soon enter into the joy of her Lord, Monnica, struck by the inspired words of her son, said: "Son, what has befallen me? Nothing has any more charms for me in this life. What I am yet to do here, and why I am here, I do not know, every hope of this world being now consumed. Once there was a reason why I should wish to live longer, that I might see you a believing Christian * before I die. God has now richly granted me this beyond measure, in permitting me to see you in His service, having totally abandoned the world. What yet have I to do here ?"

Ary Scheffer, the French painter, of the romantic school, has fixed on this sublime moment of elevation to the beatific vision for his famous and beautiful, though somewhat sentimental picture of Monnica and her son.

> "Together 'neath the Italian heaven
> They sit, the mother and her son,
> He late from her by errors riven,
> Now both in Jesus one:
> The dear consenting hands are knit,
> And either face, as there they sit,
> Is lifted as to something seen
> Beyond the blue serene."

Five or six days after this conversation and foretaste of the eternal Sabbath-rest of the saints, the pious mother was attacked by a fever, which in a short time

---

* Or more strictly, after the original. *Confess.* IX. 10, *Christianum catholicum,* " a *Catholic* (or *orthodox*) Christian," in distinction not merely from a *Paganus,* but also and particularly from a *Christianus hæreticus* and *schismaticus,* which Augustin had formerly been.

exhausted her vital powers. Her two sons were continually at her bedside. Augustin was now indeed more than ever bowed down with grief that he had caused her so many tears and pains, and sought, by the last tender offices of love, to make as much amends as possible. Monnica read his heart, and assured him with tender affection that he had never spoken an unkind word to her. Before, it had always been her wish to die at home and rest beside the grave of her husband. But now this natural wish was merged into loftier resignation to the will of God : " Bury my body somewhere here," said she, " and do not concern yourselves on its account ; only this I beg of you, that you will be mindful of me at the altar of God, where you will be." * To the question, whether it would not be terrible to her to be buried so far from her fatherland, she replied : " Nothing is far from God ; and there is no fear that He will not know at the end of time where to raise me up."

Thus, in the fifty-sixth year of her age, on the ninth day of her sickness, this noble-hearted woman expired in the arms of her son, at the mouth of the Tiber, on the shore of the Mediterranean Sea, which separated Italy from the land of her birth. Yet, long after her death, has she consoled and comforted thousands of anxious mothers and encouraged them in patient waiting and perseverance in prayer. Her memory remains forever dear and blessed to the Christian world.†

---

* *Confess.* IX. 11 : " *Tantum illud vos rogo, ut ad Domini altare meminerilis mei, ubi fueritis.*" This thanksgiving and prayer for the dead can be traced, in its innocent form, as far back as the second century, and became the fruitful germ of the doctrine of purgatory. Neither Monnica nor Augustin grasped the full meaning of St. Paul's assurance that it is " very far better to be with Christ " (Phil. i 23).

† In an epitaph of Bassus, ex-Consul, dating from the early part of the fifth century, Monnica is addressed as " Mother of Virtues," and

Adeodatus cried aloud. Augustin himself could scarcely restrain by force the gush of tears and quiet the overpowering feelings of grief which were rushing into his heart. He believed it was not becoming "to honor such a corpse with the tearful wailings and groans which are usually given to those who die a miserable—yea, an eternal death." For his mother had not died miserably: she had merely entered into the joy of her Lord. When the weeping had subsided, his friend Evodius took up the psalter: "I will sing of mercy and judgment; unto Thee, O Lord, will I sing" (Ps. ci. 1); and the whole house joined in the response.

After the corpse had been buried, and the holy Supper celebrated on the grave, according to the custom of the age, in the consciousness of a communion of saints uninterrupted by death, Augustin, finding himself at home alone with his God, gave his tears free vent, and wept sorely and long over her who had shed so many tears of maternal love and solicitude on his account. But he begs his readers to fulfil the last wish of his mother, and remember her at the altar of the Lord with thanksgiving and prayer. "In this transitory life let them remember my parents with pious affection, and my brothers, who, under Thee, the Father, are children in the mother, the Catholic Church, and my fellow-citizens in the heavenly Jerusalem, after which Thy people sigh

---

Augustin as her yet "happier offspring." This shows the early reverence paid to her memory. See the epitaph in Brieger's "Zeitschrift für Kirchengeschichte," vol. 1, p. 228. Monnica is a saint in the Roman calendar, April 4 (*Sancta Monica vidua*). Her bones were translated from Ostia to Rome in 1430 under Pope Martin V., and deposited in a chapel dedicated to Augustin. She often appears in mediæval pictures; especially famous is Ary Scheffer's *St. Augustin et sa mère Ste. Monique* (1845). It is in the same style as his Dante and Beatrice.

from the beginning to the end of their pilgrimage, so that what she asked of me in her last moments may be more abundantly fulfilled to her by the prayers and confessions of many, than by my prayers alone." *

These words are taken from the conclusion of the historical part of the *Confessions*, in which Augustin, with the rarest candor and in a spirit of the severest self-criticism and unfeigned humility, in presence of the whole world, acknowledges to God his sins and errors, and praises, with devout gratitude, the wonderful hand which, even in his widest wanderings, guided him, took hold of him, in the anxiety and prayers of his mother, in the better inclinations of his heart, in his internal conflicts, his increasing discontent, and his pining after God, and led him at last, after many storms, into the haven of faith and peace. In this autobiography we behold the great Church-doctor of all ages "lying in the dust of humility in converse with God and basking in the sunlight of His love, his readers only sweeping before him like shadows." He takes all his glory, all his greatness, all his culture, and lays them devoutly at the feet of free grace. His deepest feeling is—"All that is good in me is Thy ordering and Thy gift; all that is evil is my guilt and my judgment." No motive, drawn from anything without, prompted him to this public confession. It sprang from the innermost impulse of his soul. "I believe," says he, "and therefore I speak, as Thou, Lord, knowest. Have I not confessed my guilt before Thee, and hast Thou not forgiven the sins of my soul? Never will I excuse or justify myself before Thee, who art Truth itself; no, I will not justify myself before Thee; for if Thou art strict to mark iniquity, who can stand?"

---

* *Confess.* IX. 13, conclusion.

Most touching is his sad complaint that he was converted to the Lord so late in life, since one single hour of communion with Him is worth more than all the joys of the world besides. "I have loved Thee late, whose beauty is as old as eternity, and yet so new; I have loved Thee late. And lo! Thou wert within, but I was without, and sought Thee there. And amid Thy beautiful creation I covered myself with loathsomeness, for Thou wert with me, and I not in Thee. The external world held me far from Thee, though it were not, if I were not in Thee. Thou didst call loud and louder, and break through my deafness; Thou didst beam down bright and brighter, and overcome my blindness; Thou didst breathe, and I recovered breath and life again, and breathed in Thee. I would taste Thee, and hungered and thirsted. Thou didst touch me, and, burning, I longed after Thy peace. If ever I may live in Thee, with all that is in me, then will pain and trouble leave me; filled wholly with Thee, all within me will be life."

CHAPTER XX.

SECOND VISIT TO ROME, AND RETURN TO AFRICA.

In consequence of the death of his mother Augustin changed his plan of travel, and went, first of all, with his company to Rome, where he remained ten months.

During this time he publicly attacked his former friends, the Manichæans. He was better fitted than any one of his contemporaries for confuting their errors. "I could not," says he, in his *Retractions*, "bear in silence that the Manichæans should delude the ignorant, through boasting, by their false, deceptive abstemiousness and moderation ; and elevate themselves even above true Christians, with whom they are not worthy to be compared ; and so I wrote two books, the one on the Morals of the Catholic Church, the other on the Morals of the Manichæans."

Toward autumn of the year 388, he sailed to Africa, and, after a transient stay in Carthage with his friend Innocentius, a godly man, who had just then been delivered by prayer from a dangerous sickness, he proceeded to a country-seat near Tagaste, which, along with other real estate, he had inherited from his father. In literal obedience to the command of Christ to the rich young man (Matt. xix. 21), and in imitation of the example of many saints of previous ages, he sold his possessions and gave the proceeds to the poor, retaining, as it appears, his dwelling and the necessary means of subsistence.

Here he lived with his friends three years in a complete community of goods, retired from the world, in prayer, study, and meditation. He was, however, frequently interrupted by the inhabitants of the city asking counsel about their spiritual and temporal affairs. Numerous philosophical, polemical, and theological writings are the fruits of this sojourn in the country.

In the year 391 Augustin was called by an imperial commissioner to the Numidian seaport, Hippo Regius, the Bona of our time. He is yet known among the natives of that place as "The Great Christian" (Rumi Kebir). Hippo was destroyed by the Vandals soon after Augustin's death. Since the French conquest of Algiers it was rebuilt, and is now one of the finest towns in North Africa, numbering over ten thousand inhabitants— French, Moors, and Jews. A monument was erected to Augustin, his bronze statue on a pedestal of white marble. On the summit of the hill is a large Catholic charitable institution, where possibly may have been his garden, from which, looking out to the sea and up to heaven, he mused on "the City of God."

CHAPTER XXI.

AUGUSTIN PRIEST AND BISHOP OF HIPPO.

Having arrived at Hippo, he was forced into public office against his will. For, on one occasion, as he was listening to a sermon of the Bishop Valerius, a native of Greece, and the latter remarked that the congregation needed a priest, the people cried out for Augustin.

He was amazed, and burst into tears, for he did not wish to give up his peaceful, ascetic and literary retirement, and did not consider himself qualified for the responsible station. He followed, however, the guidance of that Hand which drew him, as it does every true reformer, into the arena of public life against his own inclination. He only begged for some months to prepare for the solemn office, and assumed its duties on Easter of the year 392.

His relation to the bishop was very pleasant. Valerius acknowledged the decided intellectual superiority of Augustin, and, without envy, gave it free play for the public good. He allowed him to preach frequently, contrary to the usual custom of the African bishops, who granted this privilege to the priests only during their absence. Soon after he made him an associate, with the consent of the Bishop of Carthage. But when Augustin learned the existence of a decree of the Council of Nicæa, forbidding two bishops in one congregation, he had a resolution passed by a Synod of Carthage that, in order to prevent similar irregularities, the Church canons should be read by every clergyman before ordination.

In the year 395, Valerius died, and Augustin was now sole Bishop of Hippo, and remained so till the day of his death. He says in one of his Epistles: "So exceedingly did I dread the episcopate that, because my reputation had now begun to be of some account among the servants of God, I would not go to any place where I knew there was no bishop. I did what I could that in a low place I might be saved, lest in a high one I should be perilled. But the servant must not oppose his Master. I came to this city to see a friend whom I thought I might gain to God, that he might live with us in the monastery; I came as being safe, the place having a bishop already. I was laid hold of, made a presbyter, and by this step came to the episcopate."

In this position he was now to unfold, during a period of thirty-eight successive years, first as priest, and then as bishop, the rich treasures of his genius for the benefit of the congregation, and the whole Church in his age and all coming centuries. He was indispensable. Difficulties of deep and universal importance were arising, with which he alone was fitted to cope.

Erasmus complains that the powers of Augustin were wasted upon Africa, and thinks that he might have produced still nobler fruits in Italy or Gaul. He was mistaken. Africa presented at the time a strange mixture of native barbarism, imported civilization of the Romans, Christianity, and lingering heathenism, not unlike the present aspect of French Algiers or British East India. Aruspices still offered sacrifices. Riotous feasts of heathen idols were nominally changed into services in honor of Christian martyrs. The Christian forces were divided. The Donastist Schismatics were almost as numerous as the Catholics, and the Manichæan heretics, not to mention smaller sects, were spread over all the cities. It was no rare thing to find even in a smaller town three rival bishops—Catholic, Donatist, and Manichæan. But it was just in conflict with these antagonistic elements that Augustin's genius developed its resources; and in contrast with the surrounding vices and signs of approaching decay his virtue and piety shine with the greater lustre. Such a man belongs to the world at large and to all ages.

CHAPTER XXII.

AUGUSTIN'S DOMESTIC LIFE.

WE will now first glance at Augustin's private life, then consider him as bishop, and lastly exhibit his public activity in the Church and the world of letters, and its influence upon succeeding generations.

His mode of living was very simple, and bore that ascetic character which accords rather with the genius of Catholicism than of Protestantism; but it was also free from narrow bigotry and Pharisaical self-righteousness, which connect themselves so readily with monastic piety.

He dwelt with his clergy in one house, and strove with them to copy after the first community of Christians (Acts iv. 31). All things were common: no one had more than another; even he himself was never preferred. God and His Church were enough for them.

Whoever would not consent to this was not admitted into his clerical body.

He was extremely sparing in his diet, and lived mostly on herbs and pulse. After the custom of those countries, wine was placed before all, a certain measure to each, yet of course further indulgence was severely rebuked. While they sat at table a passage from some good book was read aloud, or they conversed freely together, but were never allowed to attack the character of any one who was absent. Augustin enforced the observance of this rule of brotherly love very strictly. His clothing and house furniture were decent, without show or luxury. He was particularly prudent in regard to the female sex, for he permitted no woman, not even his nearest relative, to live in the episcopal house. Nor did he trust himself to enter into conversation with any, except in the presence of an ecclesiastic. Personally he preferred, like St. Paul and most of the Fathers, the unmarried estate (1 Cor. vii. 1, 7, 8). In this he must be judged by the ascetic standard of the early Church, which, in opposition to heathen immorality, went to the opposite extreme of an overestimate of virginity as a higher form of virtue than chastity in married life.

He also established a kind of theological seminary, where candidates could prepare themselves in a practical as well as theoretical manner, for their important duties as preachers of the Gospel. They certainly could find no better instructor. Already as a priest he had attracted to Hippo his old friends Alypius and Evodius, and several new ones, among whom were Possidius and Severus, for the prosecution of mutual studies, and these formed the beginning of that theological nursery out of which ten bishops and many inferior clergy went forth from time to time.

CHAPTER XXIII.

ADMINISTRATION OF THE EPISCOPAL OFFICE AND PUBLIC ACTIVITY.

As a bishop, Augustin was pre-eminently faithful and conscientious in the discharge of his manifold duties. He felt deeply the solemn responsibilities of the spiritual calling. "There is nothing," says he, "in this life, and especially in this age, more easy, more agreeable, and more acceptable to men than the office of bishop or presbyter or deacon, if its duties are performed at pleasure and in a time-serving spirit; but in the eyes of God nothing more miserable, more sad, more damnable. Likewise, there is nothing in this life, and especially in this age, more difficult, more laborious, more dangerous than the office of bishop or presbyter or deacon, but also more blessed before God, if a man conducts himself therein as a true soldier under the banner of Christ." *

To the ministry of the Word he applied himself diligently, preaching often five days in succession, and on some days twice. Whenever he found time he prepared himself for it. When, out of the fulness of inspiration he spoke from the holy place, he felt that human language was insufficient to express, in a fit and lively man-

---

* *Ep.* 21, tom. xi. ed. Bened. Words well worthy of being pondered on by every candidate of Theology. "*Nihil est in hac vita, et maxime hoc tempore, facilius et laetius et hominibus acceptabilius episcopi, aut presbyteri, aut diaconi officio, si perfunctorie atque adulatorie res agatur; sed nihil apud Deum miserius et tristius et damnabilius. Item nihil est in hac vita, et maxime in hoc tempore, difficilius, laboriosius, periculosius episcopi, aut presbyteri, aut diaconi officio; sed apud Deum nihil beatius, si eo modo militetur, quo noster imperator jubet.*"

ner, the thoughts and feelings which streamed through his soul with the speed of lightning. He set before him as the aim of spiritual oratory to preach himself and his hearers into Christ, so that all might live with him and he with all in Christ. This was his passion, his honor, his boast, his joy, his riches.

He frequently spent whole days in bringing about a reconciliation between parties who were at variance. It was irksome to a man of his contemplative disposition, but a sense of duty rendered him superior to the disagreeable nature of the occupation. He speaks of "the perplexities of other people's differences in secular matters," which he was asked to decide or to adjust by mediation; and alludes to "innumerable other ecclesiastical toils, which no one perhaps believes who has not tried." Like Ambrose, he often interceded with the authorities in behalf of the unfortunate, and procured for them either justice or mercy. He took the poor under his special care, and looked upon each clergyman as their father. Once, when he observed that but little was cast into the collection-boxes, he concluded his sermon with the words: "I am a beggar for beggars, and take pleasure in being so, in order that you may be numbered among the children of God." Like Ambrose, he even melted up the vessels of the sanctuary, in extreme cases, for the relief of the suffering and the redemption of the prisoner. Unlike many bishops of his time, he does not seem to have set his heart upon the enrichment of the Church. He would accept no legacy where injustice would be done to the natural heirs, for "the Church desires no unrighteous inheritance;" and therefore he praised Bishop Aurelius, of Carthage, in a sermon, because he had restored, without solicitation, his entire property to a man who had willed it to the Church, and whose wife had afterward unexpectedly borne him children.

Along with his seminary for the clergy he also established religious societies for women. Over one of these his sister, a godly widow, presided. On one occasion he assured his congregation that he could not easily find better, but had also nowhere found worse people than in these cloisters.

But the activity of Augustin extended beyond the limits of his own congregation, and reached the entire African—yea, the entire Western Church. He was the leading genius of the African Synods, which were held toward the close of the fourth and the beginning of the fifth century, at Carthage, A.D. 397, 403, 411, 413, 419, and in other places, particularly against the Donatists and Pelagians. He took the liveliest interest in all the questions which were then agitated, and was unwearied in devoting his powers to the general good.

The Catholic Church had at that time three great enemies, who threatened to deface and tear her in pieces at every point, and had even forced themselves into the congregation of Hippo. These were Manichæism, Donatism, and Pelagianism. Augustin was their great opponent and final conqueror. The whole spiritual power of the Latin Church concentrated itself, so to speak, in him for the overthrow of these antagonists. He left no lawful means unemployed for the expulsion of the evil. But he principally fought with the weapon of argument, and wrote a large number of works which, although designed specially for the necessities and circumstances of the time, yet contain a store of profound truths for all ages.

CHAPTER XXIV.

LAST YEARS AND DEATH.

In his latter years Augustin cast one more glance behind upon his entire literary course, and in his *Retractions* subjected it to a severe criticism. His writings against the Semi-Pelagians, in which a milder and more gentle spirit reigns, belong to this period. Like Luther and Melanchthon, he was inclined to melancholy with the failure of his bodily strength. This was increased by much bitter experience and the heavy misfortunes which befell his fatherland.

The Vandal king, Genseric, with fifty thousand warriors, among whom were Goths and Alani, in May of the year 428, crossed over from Spain to Africa, which was now filled with confusion and desolation. These barbarians raged more fiercely than wild beasts of prey, reduced towns and villages to ashes, spared no age or sex, were especially severe against the orthodox clergy, because they themselves were Arians, and changed that beautiful country into a desert.

Augustin was of the opinion that the bishops at least should stand by their congregations in the hour of need, that the bonds which the love of Christ had knit should not be rent asunder, and that they should endure quietly whatever God might send. "Whoever flies," he wrote to Bishop Quodvultdeus, "so that the Church is not deprived of the necessary ministrations, he does what God commands or permits. But whoever so flies that the flock of Christ is left without the nourishment by which it spiritually lives, he is an hireling, who, seeing the wolf come, flies because he has no care for the sheep."

Boniface, the commander-in-chief of the imperial forces in Africa, who was friendly to Augustin, though the occasion of much trouble to him, was beaten by the Vandals, and threw himself with the remnant of his army into the fortified city of Hippo, where Possidius and several other bishops had taken refuge. Augustin was sorely oppressed by the calamities of his country and the destruction of divine worship, which could now be celebrated only in the strongholds of Carthage, Cirta, and Hippo. At table he once expressed himself to his friends in the following language : " What I pray God for is that He will deliver this city from the enemy, or if He has determined otherwise, that He may strengthen His servant for his sufferings, or, which I would rather, that He will call me from this world to Himself."

The last wish was granted him. In the third month of the siege he was attacked by a violent fever, and ten days before his death he withdrew into retirement, after having, up till that time, proclaimed the Word of God to his congregation without interruption. He spent this season in reading the penitential psalms, which were attached to the wall by his bedside, in holy meditations, tears, prayers, and intercessions. He once said that no one, especially no priest, ought to depart this life without earnest repentance, and wrote concerning himself : " I will not cease to weep until He comes, and I appear before Him, and these tears are to me pleasant nutriment. The thirst which consumes me, and incessantly draws me toward yon fountain of my life—this thirst is always more burning when I see my salvation delayed. This inextinguishable desire carries me away to those streams, as well amid the joys as amid the sorrows of this world. Yea, if I stand well with the world I am wretched in myself, until I appear before God."

On the 28th of August, 430, in the seventy-sixth year of his age, the great man peacefully departed into a blissful eternity, in the full possession of his faculties, and in the presence of his friends.

He left no will, for, having embraced voluntary poverty, he had nothing to dispose of, except his books and manuscripts, which he bequeathed to the Church.*

Soon after Hippo was taken. Henceforth Africa was lost to the Romans, and vanished from the arena of Church History. The culminating point of the spiritual greatness of the African Church was also that of her ruin. But her ripest fruit, the spirit and the theology of Augustin, could not perish. It fell on the soil of Europe, where it has produced new glorious flowers and fruits, and to this day exerts a mighty influence in Catholic and Protestant Christendom.

CHAPTER XXV.

AUGUSTIN'S WRITINGS.

AUGUSTIN is the most fruitful author among the Latin Church-Fathers. His writings are almost too numerous. One of his biographers reckons them, including about four hundred sermons and two hundred and seventy letters, at ten hundred and thirty. Others reduce the whole

---

* His friend and biographer, Possidius, says, *Vit. Aug.* c. 31 : " *Testamentum nullum fecit, quia unde faceret, pauper Dei non habuit. Ecclesiæ bibliothecam omnesque codices diligenter posteris custodiendos semper jubebat.*"

number to two hundred and thirty-two, and the larger ones to ninety-three. They fill eleven folio volumes in the Benedictine edition of Augustin's works.*

They contain his views in every department of theology, the rare treasures of his mind and heart, and a true expression of the deepest religious and churchly movements of his age, and at the same time secured an immeasurable influence upon all succeeding generations. He wrote out of the abundance of his heart, not to acquire literary fame, but moved by the love of God and man.

In point of learning he stands far behind Origen, Eusebius, and Jerome; but in originality, depth, and wealth of thought he surpasses all the Greek and Latin Fathers. He knew no Hebrew and very little Greek, as he modestly confesses himself.† He neglected and disliked the noble language of Hellas in his youth, because he had a bad teacher, and was forced to it. But after his conversion, during his second residence in Rome, he resumed the study of it, and acquired a sufficient elementary knowledge to compare the Latin version of the Scriptures with the Septuagint and the Greek Testament.‡

---

* A considerable number of them have been translated into English, especially the *Confessions*, and the *City of God*. See the Oxford "Library of the Fathers," 1837 sqq.; "Works of Aurelius Augustine," ed. by Marcus Dods, D.D., Edinburgh, 1871–1876, 15 vols.; and Schaff's edition, New York, 1886–88, 8 vols.

† "*Græcæ linguæ perparum assecutus sum, et prope nihil.*" *Contra Literas Petiliani* II. 38. Comp. *De Trinitate* III. Prooem.; *Confess.* I. 14; VII. 9.

‡ He gives the etymology of several Greek words, as αἰώνιον, ἀνάθεμα, ἐγκαίνια, λόγος, etc.; he correctly distinguishes between γεννᾶν and τίκτειν, ἐνταφιάζειν and θάπτειν, εὐχή and προσευχή, πνοή and πνεῦμα. He amends the *Itala* in about thirty places from the Septuagint, and in three places from the Greek Testament (John

Gibbon, usually very accurate, underestimates him when he says that "the superficial learning of Augustin was confined to the Latin language," and that "his style, though sometimes animated by the eloquence of passion, is usually clouded by false and affected rhetoric."* The judgment of Dr. Baur, who had as little sympathy with Augustin's theology, but a far better knowledge of it, is more just and correct : " There is scarcely another theological author so fertile and withal so able as Augustin. His scholarship was certainly not equal to his genius ; yet even that is sometimes set too low, when it is asserted that he had no acquaintance at all with the Greek language ; for this is incorrect, though he had attained no great proficiency in Greek." †

---

viii. 25 ; xviii. 37 ; Rom. i. 3). He also corrects Julian, his Pelagian antagonist, by going back to the Greek. He explains the Greek monogram ἰχθύς (*De Civ. Dei* xviii. 23). He mentions the opinion (*De Civ. Dei* xx. 19) that in 2 Thess. ii. 4 we should render the Greek (εἰς τὸν ναὸν τοῦ θεοῦ), not *in templo Dei*, but more correctly *in templum Dei*, as if Antichrist and his followers were themselves the temple of God, the Church. He probably read Plotinus and Porphyry in the original. Comp. Loesche : *De Augustino Plotinizante in doctrina de Deo*, Jena, 1880.

* *Decline and Fall*, Ch. XXXIII. He adds that "Augustin possessed a strong, capacious, argumentative mind ; he boldly sounded the abyss of grace, predestination, free will, and original sin ; and the rigid system of Christianity which he framed or restored has been entertained with public applause and secret reluctance by the Catholic Church." He says in a note : "The Church of Rome has canonized Augustin and reprobated Calvin."

† *Dogmengesch.* I. 1, p. 61 ; comp the section on Augustin in the second volume of Baur's *Church History.* Compare also the judgments of Villemain, *Tableau de l'éloquence chrétienne au IVe siècle*, Paris, 1849, p. 373 ; of Ozanam, *La civilization au cinquième siècle* (vol. I. 272, in Glyn's translation); and the eloquent account of the veteran and liberal historian, Karl Hase, in the first volume of his *Lectures on Church History*, Leipzig, 1885, vol. I. 514 sqq.

His style may indeed be blamed for verbosity, negligence, and frequent repetition, but he says : " I would rather be censured by the grammarians than not understood by the people ;" and, upon the whole, he had the language wholly at command, and knew how to wield the majestic power, the dignity and music of the Latin in a masterly manner. His writings are full of ingenious puns, and rise not seldom to strains of true eloquence and poetic beauty. Several of his pregnant sentences have become permanently lodged in the memory of the Christian world. Such words of genius and wisdom engraven upon the rock are worth more than whole libraries written upon the sand. The following are among his most striking and suggestive thoughts :

Cor nostrum inquietum est donec requiescat in Te.
Our heart is restless until it rests in Thee.
Novum Testamentum in Vetere latet, Vetus in Novo patet.
The New Testament is concealed in the Old, the Old is revealed in the New.
Ubi amor ibi trinitas.
Where love is there is trinity.
Distingue tempora, et concordabit Scriptura.
Distinguish the times, and the Scriptures will agree.
Da quod jubes, et jube quod vis.
Give what Thou commandest, and command what Thou wilt.
Fides præcedit intellectum.
Faith precedes knowledge.
Non vincit nisi veritas ; victoria veritatis est caritas.
Truth only is victorious ; the victory of truth is charity.
Nulla infelicitas frangit, quem felicitas nulla corrumpit.
No misfortune can break him whom no fortune corrupts.
Deo servire vera libertas est.
To serve God is true liberty.

To Augustin is also popularly but falsely ascribed the famous and beautiful device of Christian union :

In necessariis unitas, in dubiis libertas, in omnibus caritas.
In essentials unity, in non-essentials liberty, in all things charity.

This sentence cannot be found in his writings. It is too liberal for a Catholic divine, and is probably of Protestant origin. It has been traced to Rupert Meldenius and Richard Baxter, two irenical divines of the seventeenth century, one a German Lutheran or Melanchthonian, the other an English Presbyterian, who in the midst of the fury of theological controversies grew sick of strife and longed after union and peace.

Since his productive period as an author extends over four decades of years, from his conversion to the evening of his life, and since he unfolded himself before the eyes of the public, contradictions on many minor points were unavoidable; wherefore, in old age, he subjected his literary career to a conscientious revision in his *Retractions*, and, in a spirit of genuine Christian humility, recalled much that he had maintained before from honest conviction. But not all his changes are improvements. He had more liberal views in his younger years.

His philosophical writings, which were composed soon after his conversion, and which are yet full of Platonism, we have already mentioned.

His theological works may be divided into five classes :*

1. Exegetical Writings. Here we may name his Expositions of the Sermon on the Mount (393), of the Epistle to the Galatians (394), of the Psalms (415), of John (416), his Harmony of the Gospels (400), and an extensive commentary on the first three chapters of Genesis (415).

His strength lies not in knowledge of the original lan-

---

* For a fuller account see the author's *Church History*, vol. III. (revised ed. 1884), p. 1005 sqq. For his philosophical works and opinions the reader is referred to Ritter, Erdmann, Ueberweg, Nourrison, Gangauf, and A. Dorner, mentioned there, p. 989 and 1039.

guages, nor in historical and grammatical exegesis, in which he was excelled by Jerome among the Latins, and Chrysostom, Theodoret, and Theophylact among the Greeks, but in the development of theological and religious thought. He depended mostly on the imperfect *Itala*, which was current before Jerome's Vulgate. Hence he often misses the natural sense. But he had an uncommon familiarity and full inward sympathy with the Holy Scriptures, and often penetrates their deepest meaning by spiritual intuition. He is ingenious and suggestive, even where he violates the grammar or loses himself in allegorical fancies. He exercised also a considerable influence on the final settlement of the canon of Holy Scripture, whose limit was so firmly fixed at the Synods of Hippo in the year 393, and of Carthage in 397, that even now it is universally received in the Catholic and Evangelical churches, with the exception of a difference in regard to the value of the Old Testament Apocrypha, which the Council of Trent included in the Canon, while the Protestant Confessions exclude them or assign them a subordinate position.

2. APOLOGETIC Writings. To these belong pre-eminently his twenty-two books on the " City of God " (*De Civitate Dei*), begun in 413 and finished in 426, in the seventy-second year of his life. It is his most learned and influential work. It is a noble and genial defence of Christianity and the Church, in the face of the approaching downfall of the old Roman Empire and classic civilization, in the face of the irruption of the wild, northern barbarians into Southern Europe and Africa, and in the face of the innumerable misfortunes and calamities by which the human race was scourged during that transition-period, and which were attributed by the heathen to the decay of the ancient faith in the gods,

and laid to the charge of Christianity. Augustin shows that all these events are the result of a process of internal putrefaction long since begun, a judgment to the heathen, and a powerful call on them to awake and repent, and at the same time a healthful trial to Christians, and the birth-throes of a new spiritual creation. Then he turns from the view of a perishing natural world and her representative, the city of Rome, conquered and laid waste by Alaric, the King of the Goths, in the year 410, to the contemplation of a higher, supernatural world—to the City of God, founded by Christ upon a rock; this city can never be destroyed, but out of all the changes and revolutions of time must rise, phœnix-like, with new power and energy; and after the fulfilment of her earthly mission shall be separated even from external communion with the world, and enter into the Sabbath of eternal rest and spiritual repose. "The City of God" is the first attempt at a philosophy of history, viewed under the aspect of two antagonistic kingdoms.

3. DOGMATIC and POLEMIC Works. These are very numerous and important. Augustin was particularly endowed as a speculative divine, a powerful reasoner, and an acute controversialist. There is scarcely a theological question which he did not revolve in his mind over and over again. He ascended the highest heights and sounded the deepest depths of religious speculation. His opinions are always worth considering. He had very strong convictions, but was free from passion, and never indulged in personalities. He was forcible in matter and sweet in spirit, and spoke "the truth in love."

Among his dogmatic works we mention the fifteen books on the Holy Trinity (against the Arians); the hand-book (*Enchiridion*) on Faith, Hope, and Love; and the four books on Christian doctrine (*De Doctrina*

Christiana), a hermeneutic dogmatic compendium for religious teachers, and instruction in the development of Christian doctrine from the Holy Scripture.

His polemic treatises may again be divided into three classes:

(*a*) *Anti-Manichæan* Writings: "On the Morals of the Manichæans;" on the "Morals of the Catholic Church;" on "Free Will;" on the "Two Souls;" "Against Faustus," and others. They are the chief source of our knowledge of the Manichæan errors, and their refutation. They belong to his earliest works. They defend the freedom of will against fatalism; afterwards he changed his opinion on that subject.

(*b*) *Anti-Donatistic* Writings: "On Baptism against the Donatists;" "Against the Epistle of Parmenianus;" "Against Petilianus;" "Extract from the Transactions of the Religious Conference with the Donatists;" and others. They are the chief source of our knowledge of the remarkable Donatistic schism in Africa, which began long before Augustin's time, and was overcome principally by his intellectual ability. They treat chiefly of the essence and the attributes of the Church and her relation to the world, of the evil of schism and separation. They complete the development of the Catholic idea of the Church, her visible unity and universality, which was begun already by Ignatius and Irenæus, and carried on by Cyprian. They were composed between 393 and 420.

Unfortunately he approved also of coercive measures of state for the suppression of the separatistic movement, and supported it by a false exegesis of the passage, "Compel them to come in" (Luke xiv. 23). He thus furnished the chief authority in the middle ages for those cruel persecutions of heretics which blacken so many pages of Church History, and from which, if he could have foreseen them, his own Christian feelings would have shrunk back in horror. Thus great and good men, even without intending it, have, through mistaken zeal, occasioned much mischief.

(c) *Anti-Pelagian* Writings, of the years 411–420, to which are to be added the *anti-Semi-Pelagian* writings of the last years of his life. We mention here the books "On Nature and Grace;" "On Merit and Forgiveness;" "On Grace and Free-Will;" "On the Spirit and the Letter;" "On Original Sin;" "On the Predestination of the Saints;" "On the Gift of Perseverance" (*De Dono Perseverantiæ*); "Against Pelagius and Cœlestius;" "Against Julian" (a bishop of Eclanum in Apulia, infected with Pelagianism). In these treatises Augustin develops his profound doctrines of original sin, the natural inability of man for good; of the grace and merit of Christ; of eternal election; of faith and perseverance to the end—in opposition to the shallow and superficial errors of the contemporaneous monks, Pelagius and Cœlestius, who denied natural depravity, and just so far overthrew the value of divine grace in Christ.

These books belong to his most meritorious labors, and are decidedly evangelical, though not free from exaggerations. They have exerted a greater influence on the Reformers of the sixteenth century, especially on Luther, Melanchthon, and Calvin, than any of his own or of all other human productions besides.* His anti-Pelagian views of sin and grace and divine foreordination are technically called "the Augustinian system," and this

---

* I furnished a detailed representation of the Pelagian controversy and Augustin's views in connection with it for the "Bibliotheca Sacra and Theological Review" of Andover for the year 1848, vol. v., p. 205-243, and in my *Church History*, vol. III., 783-865.

again is often, though erroneously, identified with the Calvinistic system of theology. But he held along with it other views which are essentially Catholic and un-protestant, especially on the Church, on baptism, on justification, on asceticism.

4. ASCETIC and PRACTICAL Writings. Among these we may number the "Soliloquies;" "Meditations;" "On the Christian Conflict;" "On the Excellency of Marriage," and a great mass of sermons and homilies, part of which were written out by himself and part taken down by his hearers. Of these there are about four hundred, besides those which that indefatigable editor of unpublished manuscripts, Cardinal Angelo Mai, has discovered among the treasures of the Vatican Library, and given to the press.

5. AUTOBIOGRAPHICAL, or writings which concern his own life and personal relations. Here belong the invaluable "Confessions," already known to us—his exhibition of himself to the time of his conversion; the "Retractions," his revision and self-correcting retrospect at the close of his splendid career in the Church and the fields of literature; lastly, a collection of two hundred and seventy letters, in which he exhibits a true picture of his external and internal life.

CHAPTER XXVI.

THE INFLUENCE OF AUGUSTIN ON HIS OWN AND SUCCEEDING GENERATIONS.

FROM this comprehensive mass of writings it is easy to determine the significance and influence of Augustin.

In the sphere of theology, as well as in all other spheres of literature, it is not the quantity, but the quality of the intellectual product which renders it most effective. The apostles have written but little; and yet the Gospel of St. John, for example, or the Epistle to the Romans exert more influence than whole libraries of excellent books—yea, than the literatures of whole nations. Tertullian's "Apology;" Cyprian's short treatise on the "Unity of the Church;" Anselm's "*Cur Deus homo*," and "*Monologium;*" Bernhard's tracts on "Despising the World," and on "The Love of God;" the anonymous little book of "German Theology," and similar productions, which may be contained in a couple of sheets, have moved and blessed more minds than the numerous abstruse folio volumes of many scholastics of the Middle Ages and old Protestant divines. Augustin's "Confessions;" the simple little book of the humble, secluded monk, Thomas à Kempis, on the "Imitation of Christ;" Bunyan's "Pilgrim's Progress;" Arndt's "True Christianity," have each converted, edified, strengthened, and consoled more persons than whole ship-loads of indifferent religious books and commentaries.

But Augustin was not only a voluminous writer, but also a profound thinker and subtle reasoner. His books, with all the faults and repetitions of isolated parts, are a spontaneous outflow from the marvellous treasures of his highly-gifted mind and his truly pious heart. Although he occupied one of the smaller bishoprics, he was yet, in fact, the head and leading spirit of the African Church, around whom Aurelius of Carthage, the primate of Africa, Evodius of Uzala, Fortunatus of Cirta, Possidius of Calama, Alypius of Tagaste, and many other bishops willingly and gladly ranged themselves—yea, in him the whole Western Church of antiquity reached its highest spiritual vigor and bloom. His appearance in the history of dogmas forms a distinct epoch, especially as it regards anthropological and soteriological doctrines, which he advanced considerably further, and brought to a greater clearness and precision than they had ever had before in the consciousness of the Church. For this was needed such a rare union of the speculative talent of the Greek, and of the practical spirit of the Latin Church as he alone possessed. As in the doctrines of sin and grace, of the fall of Adam and the redemption of Christ, the two cardinal points of practical Christianity, he went far beyond the theology of the Oriental Church, which devoted its chief energies to the development of the dogmas of the Holy Trinity and the person of Christ, so at the same time he opened up new paths for the progress of Western theology.

Not only over his own age, but over all succeeding generations also, he has exercised an immeasurable influence, and does still, as far as the Christian Church and theological science reach, with the exception of the Greek Church, which adheres to her own traditions and the decisions of the seven Œcumenical Councils. It may be doubted if ever any uninspired theologian has had and still has so large a number of admirers and disciples as the Bishop of Hippo. While most of the great men in the history of the Church are claimed either by the Catholic or by the Protestant Confession, and their influence is therefore confined to one or the other, he enjoys from both a respect equally profound and enduring.

On the one hand, he is among the chief creators of the *Catholic* theology. Through the whole of the Middle Ages, from Gregory the Great down to the Fathers of Trent, he was the highest theological authority. Thomas Aquinas alone could in some measure contest this rank with him. By his fondness for speculation and his dialectic acumen he became the father of mediæval *scholasticism;* and at the same time, by his devotional fervor and spirit glowing with love, the author of mediæval *mysticism.* Hence the most distinguished representatives of scholasticism—as Anselm, Peter Lombard, Thomas Aquinas—and the representatives of mysticism—as Bernhard of Clairvaux, Hugo of St. Victor, and Tauler—have collectively appealed to his authority, been nourished on his writings, and saturated with his spirit. Even at this day the Catholic Church, notwithstanding her condemnation of many doctrines of Augustin, under the names of Protestant, and Jansenist heresies, counts him among her greatest saints and most illustrious doctors.

It must not be omitted that he is responsible also for many grievous errors of the Roman Church. He advocated the principle of persecution ; he taught the damnation of unbaptized infants ; he anticipated the dogma of the immaculate conception of the Virgin Mary ; and his ominous word, *Roma locuta est, causa finita est,* might almost be quoted in favor of the Vatican decree of papal infallibility. These errors lie like an incubus on the Roman Church. Error is all the more tenacious and dangerous the greater the truth it contains, and the greater and wiser the man who advocates it.

But, on the other hand, this same Augustin has also an *evangelical-Protestant* significance. Next to the Apostle Paul, he was the chief teacher of the whole body of the Reformers of the sixteenth century, and his exegetical and anti-Pelagian writings were the main source from which they derived their views on the depravity of human nature and the excellence of the forgiving, regenerating, and sanctifying grace of God in Christ, and opposed the dead formalism, self-righteous Pelagianism, and stiff mechanism of the scholastic theology and monkish piety of that age. As is well known, they followed him from the very beginning even to the dizzy abyss of the doctrine of predestination, which Luther (in his work *De Servo Arbitrio*) and Calvin reproduced in its most rigorous form, in order to root out Pelagianism and Semi-Pelagianism, and with them all human boasting. Of Augustin they always speak with high esteem and love, which is the more remarkable because they are otherwise very free not only with the mediæval schoolmen, but with the ancient Fathers, and sometimes even, in the passionate heat of their opposition to slavish reverence, treat them with neglect and contempt.*

---

* In this, as everywhere, Luther is especially outspoken and characteristic. His contempt for Scholasticism, which he derives from "the accursed heathen Aristotle," is well known. Even the writings of Thomas Aquinas, for whom the Lutheran theologians of the seventeenth century had great respect, he once calls "the dregs of all heresies, error, and destruction of the Gospel." Neither did he spare the ancient Fathers, being conscious of the difference between Protestant and Patristic theology. "All the Fathers," he once says without ceremony, "have erred in faith, and, if not converted before death, are eternally damned." "St. Gregory is the useless fountainhead and author of the fables of purgatory and masses for souls. He

I will add the most recent estimates of Augustin by Protestant historians in confirmation of the views expressed in this chapter.

———————

was very ill acquainted with Christ and His Gospel; he is entirely too superstitious; the Devil has corrupted him." On Jerome, whose *Vulgata* was indispensable in his translation of the Bible into German, he was particularly severe on account of his monastic tendencies and legalism. He calls him a "heretic who has written much profanity. He has deserved hell more than heaven. I know no one of the Fathers to whom I am so hostile, as to him. He writes only about fasting, virginity, and such things." For the same reason he condemns St. Basil, one of the chief promoters of monachism: "He is good for nothing; is only a monk; I would not give a straw for him." Of Chrysostom, the greatest expounder of the Scriptures and pulpit-orator of the Greek Church, but of whom certainly he had only the most superficial knowledge, he says, "He is worth nothing to me; he is a babbler, wrote many books, which make a great show, but are only huge, wild, tangled heaps and crowds and bags full of words, for there is nothing in them, and little wool sticks." Nowadays not a solitary Lutheran theologian of any learning will agree with him in this view. The Reformer was at times dissatisfied with Augustin himself, because, amid all his congeniality of mind, he could not just find in him his "*sola* fide." "Augustin has often erred, he is not to be trusted. Although good and holy, he was yet lacking in true faith as well as the other Fathers." But over against this casual expression stand a number of eulogies on Augustin.

Luther's words must not be weighed too nicely, else any and everything can be proven by him, and the most irreconcilable contradictions shown. We must always judge him according to the moment and mood in which he spoke, and duly remember his bluntness and his stormy, warlike nature. Thus, the above disparaging sentences upon some of the greatest theologians are partly annulled by his churchly and historical feeling, and by many expressions, like that in a letter to Albert of Prussia (A.D. 1532), where he declares the importance of tradition in matters of faith, as strongly as any Catholic. In reference to the real presence of Christ in the Lord's Supper, he says: "Moreover this article has been unanimously believed and held from the beginning of the Christian Church to the present hour, as may be shown from the books and writings of the dear Fathers, both in the Greek and Latin languages, which testimony

Dr. Bindemann, one of the best Protestant biographers of Augustin, thus sums up his estimate of his character and influence: "Augustin is one of the most extraordinary lights in the Church. In importance he takes rank behind no teacher who has labored in her since the days of the apostles. It may well be said that the first place among the Church Fathers is due to him, and at the time of the Reformers only a Luther, by reason of the fulness and depth of his spirit and his nobleness of character, was worthy to stand at his side. He is the highest point of the development of the Western Church before the Middle Ages. From him the Mysticism, no less than the Scholasticism of the Middle Ages, has drawn its life; he forms the mightiest pillar of Roman Catholicism; and the leaders of the Reformation derived from his writings next to the study of the Holy Scriptures, especially the Paulinian Epistles, those principles which gave birth to a new era." Dr. Kurtz (in the eleventh edition of his *Church History*, 1890) calls Augustin "the greatest, mightiest, and most influential of all the fathers, from whom the entire doctrinal and ecclesiastical development of the Occident proceeded, and to whom it returns again and again in all its turning-points." Dr. Carl

---

of the entire holy Christian Church ought to be sufficient for us, even if we had nothing more. *For it is dangerous and dreadful to hear or believe anything against the unanimous testimony, faith, and doctrine of the entire holy Christian Church, as it has been held unanimously in all the world up to this year* 1500. Whoever now doubts of this, he does just as much as though he believed in no Christian Church, and condemns not only the entire holy Christian Church as a damnable heresy, but Christ Himself, and all the apostles and prophets, who founded this article, when we say, 'I believe in a holy Christian Church,' to which Christ bears powerful testimony in Matt. xxviii. 20: 'Lo I am with you always to the end of the world,' and Paul in 1 Tim. iii. 15: 'The Church is the pillar and ground of the truth.'"

Burk (in his *Church History*, 1885) says that in Augustin ancient and modern ideas are melted, and that to his authority the papal church has as much right to appeal as the churches of the Reformation. Karl Hase emphasizes the liberal features of Augustin, and remarks that " a right estimate of his importance as an author can only be made when we perceive how the scholastics and mystics of the Middle Ages lived upon his riches, and how even Luther and Calvin drew out of his depths." Harnack judges that between Paul and Luther no divine can be compared with Augustin for extent of influence.

The great genius of the African Church, from whom the Middle Ages and the Reformation have received an impulse alike powerful, though in different directions, has not yet fulfilled the work marked out for it in the counsels of Divine Wisdom. He serves as a bond of union between the two antagonistic sections of Western Christendom, and encourages the hope that a time may come when the injustice and bitterness of strife will be forgiven and forgotten, and the discords of the past be drowned forever in the sweet harmonies of perfect knowledge and perfect love.

This end may be afar off. It will come when the "City of God" is completed. "Then and there" (to use the closing words of his admirable work) "we shall rest and see, see and love, love and praise. This is what shall be in the end without end. For what other end do we propose to ourselves than to attain to the Kingdom of which there shall be no end?"

What Augustin has so beautifully said of men as individuals may, with great propriety, be applied also to the ages of the Church: "Thou, O Lord, hast created us for Thyself, and our hearts are restless until they rest in Thee."

CHAPTER XXVII.

THE AUGUSTINIAN SYSTEM.

A FEW words more on the anti-Pelagian system of Augustin, which is so closely interwoven with the history of Protestant theology. It is imbedded in the Confessions of the Reformation; it ruled the scholastic theology of the Lutheran and Reformed churches during the seventeenth century; it was gradually undermined first by the Arminian movement in Holland, then by the Wesleyan Methodism in England and America, and by the rationalistic revolution of the last century, but is still held by the schools of strict orthodoxy in the Lutheran and Calvinistic churches, with this difference, however, that the Lutheran Formula of Concord teaches a *universal call* in connection with a *particular election*, and rejects the decree of reprobation.

The Roman Church accepted Augustinianism only in part and in subordination to her sacramentarian and sacerdotal system. The Greek Church ignored it altogether, although Pelagius was condemned with Nestorius by the Œcumenical Council of Ephesus in 431, without a doctrinal statement of the controverted points.

The Augustinian system assumes but one probation of man and but one act of freedom, which was followed by a universal slavery of sin and by a partial redemption; God choosing by an eternal decree of grace from the mass of perdition a definite number of the elect for salvation, and leaving the rest to their deserved ruin. It suspends the eternal fate of Adam and his unborn posterity, which he represented, upon a single act of disobedience, which resulted in the damnation of untold millions of immortal beings, including all unbaptized infants dying in infancy. That act, with its fearful consequences, was, of course, eternally foreseen by the omniscient God, and must in some sense also have been decreed or foreordained, since nothing can happen without His sovereign and almighty will. Augustin and the Protestant Confessions stop within the *infralapsarian* scheme, which puts the fall only under a *permissive* decree, and makes Adam and the race responsible for sin. Here is an inconsistency, which has its root in a strong sense of God's holiness and man's guilt. The *supralapsarian* scheme, which was developed by a school in Calvinistic churches, but never obtained symbolical sanction, is logically more consistent, but practically more revolting by including the fall itself in an *efficient* decree of God, and making sin the necessary means for the manifestation of divine mercy in the saved, and of divine justice in the lost.

Melanchthon in his later years, and the Arminians after him, felt the speculative and moral difficulties of Augustinianism, but were no more able to remove them by their compromise theories than the Semi-Pelagians of old. Yea, even Calvin, while accepting in faith the absolute decree, called it a "*decretum horribile, attamen verum.*"

Long before Augustin, Origen had taught another solution of the problem of sin, based on the Platonic theory of pre-existence; he went even beyond the beginning of history where Augustin began, and assumed a *pre-historic* fall of every individual soul (not of the race, as Augustin held), but also a final salvation of all.

Schleiermacher combined the Augustinian or Calvinistic predestinarianism with the Origenistic restorationism, and taught a universal election, which unfolds itself by degrees, and, while involving a *temporary* reprobation of the impenitent, results in the final conversion and restoration of all men to holiness and happiness. Pantheism goes still further, and makes sin a necessary transition point in the process of moral evolution, but thereby cuts the nerve of moral responsibility, and overthrows the holiness of God.

Thus the deepest and strongest minds, both philosophers and theologians, have been wrestling again and again with the dark, terrific problem of sin and death in its relation to an all-wise, holy, and merciful God, and yet have reached no satisfactory solution except that God overrules evil for a greater good. The Augustinian system contains a vast amount of profound truth, and has trained some of the purest and strongest types of Christian character among the Jansenists and Huguenots of France, the Calvinists of Holland, the Puritans of England, the Covenanters of Scotland, and the Pilgrim Fathers of New England. Nevertheless, as a system it is unsatisfactory, because it assumes an unconscious and yet responsible pre-existence of the race in Adam, and because it leaves out of sight the *universal* benevolence and *impartial* justice of God to all His creatures, and the freedom and individual responsibility of man, who stands or falls with his own actual sins. But it will require another theological genius even deeper and broader than Origen, Augustin, Thomas Aquinas, Calvin, and Schleiermacher, to break the spell of that system by substituting a better one from the inexhaustible mines of the Scripture, which contains all the elements and aspects of the truth, without giving disproportion to one and doing injustice to another.

The study of history liberalizes and expands the mind, and teaches us to respect and love, without idolatry, every great and good man notwithstanding his errors of judgment and defects of character. There never was an unerring and perfect being on earth but One who is more than man, and who alone could say: "I am the Way, and the Truth, and the Life."

LITERATURE.

For the extensive bibliography on St. Augustin the reader is referred to Schaff's *History of the Christian Church*, vol. III., 988–90 and 1038 sq. (last revision, 1889), and the Prolegomena to his *Nicene and Post-Nicene Library*, First Series (1886–90), vol. I., 1–3.

The best edition of St. Augustin's Works, in the original Latin, is the Benedictine, Paris, 1679–1700, 11 tom. in 8 vols. fol., which has been several times reprinted—*e.g.*, by Gaume, Paris, 1836–39, and Migne, 1841–49 (in 12 vols.). The English translations have already been mentioned in Chapter XXV.

The chief biographers of St. Augustin are POSSIDIUS, his pupil and friend; POUJOULAT, in French (Paris, 1843 and 1852, 2 vols.); C. BINDEMANN, in German (Berlin, 1844–69, 3 vols.).

On his theology, see W. CUNNINGHAM: *St. Austin and his Place in Christian Thought*, Cambridge, 1886; H. REUTER: *Augustinische Studien*, Gotha, 1887; and the able critique of the Augustinian system by ADOLF HARNACK in the third volume of his *Dogmengeschichte*, Freiburg i. B., 1890, pp. 3 sqq.; 54 sqq.; 84 sqq.; 151 sqq.

The present biography is a free reproduction and enlargement of the author's *Der heil. Augustinus. Sein Leben und Wirken*, published by W. Hertz, in Berlin, 1854. An English translation by his friend, Professor Thomas C. Porter, D D., was published by J. C. Riker, New York, 1854, and Samuel Bagster & Sons, London, 1854.

THE CYCLOPÆDIA OF NATURE TEACHINGS.

WITH AN INTRODUCTION BY REV.

HUGH MACMILLAN, LL.D., F.R.S.E.,

AUTHOR OF "BIBLE TEACHINGS IN NATURE," ETC.

8vo, Cloth Extra.   Price, $2.50.   Just Out.

One of the most characteristic features of modern culture is the attention given to the facts, moods and suggestions of "Nature."

Teachers and preachers are feeling the need for illustrations from Nature in their pulpit, platform and class work, and as the scientific knowledge and the love of Nature increase in schools and in congregations, there must be an increasing demand for illustrations taken from the spheres in which audiences are becoming daily more interested.

The **Cyclopædia of Nature Teachings** is a collection of remarkable passages from the writings and utterances of the leading authors, preachers and orators, which embody suggestive or curious information concerning Nature. Each passage contains some important or noteworthy fact or statement which may serve to illustrate religious truth or moral principles, the extracts being gleaned from the widest and most varied sources.

The passages are arranged alphabetically under subjects, and subdivided so as to elucidate the topic treated of and illustrate it in every possible way. Thus under the head of THE AIR, we find on this subject passages are given on THE BEAUTY OF CLOUDS, THE MYSTERIES OF THE CLOUDS, CHANGES IN THE SKY, MISTS AND SUNSHINE, THE MESSAGE OF THE HEAVENS, SKY INFLUENCES, AUTUMN, SUNSHINE, PLANTS, THE ATMOSPHERE, etc., etc.

That the **Cyclopædia** is a work of true value and reliable information will be seen by the names of the following authors, from whose writings, among many others, some of the extracts are taken, viz., RUSKIN, JEFFERIES, MACLAREN, McCOOK, HUGH MACMILLAN, BEECHER, SMILEY, WILSON, PULSFORD, GUTHRIE, FROUDE, LYTTON, ROBERTSON, ARTHUR, ARNOT, HERSCHEL, PROCTER, FABER, TAYLOR, DAWSON, HELPS, EMERSON, DICKENS, AGASSIZ, PARKER, CONDER, CHALMERS, BALDWIN, BROWN, CUVIER, RICHTER, GOETHE, etc.

The volume forms a most valuable work of reference, and by its orderly arrangement puts its wealth of information and suggestion at the disposition of the student or teacher; but the varied character of the selections, the freshness of the subjects treated, and the literary grace of many of the paragraphs will also make the work welcome to general readers.

The **Cyclopædia of Nature Teachings** is furnished with a very copious index of subjects, and also one of Bible texts.

NEW YORK: THOMAS WHITTAKER, 2 AND 3 BIBLE HOUSE.

The Bishop Paddock Lectures for 1889.

DIABOLOLOGY.

The Person and Kingdom of Satan.

By REV. EDWARD H. JEWETT, S.T.D.,

Prof. of Pastoral Theology in the General Theological Seminary
New York.

Octavo, cloth binding. Price, $1.50.

This work is, in so far as it goes, a thorough and scholarly examination of the oft-mooted, and frequently denied doctrine of a personal devil. As stated by the author in his preface, "These lectures were written in the hope that they might contribute, in some degree at least, to the removal of error, and the firmer confirmation of faith in the important doctrines of which they treat." Although written primarily for the scholarly public, the style is simple, and the language clear and easily comprehensible by the ordinary reader. Where quotations are given as foot notes in their original languages, a translation is embodied within the text itself and on the same pages. To such as deny with the Sadducees of old, the existence of a spirit world, the arguments presented may possibly possess but little convincing power; but, to the believers in the literal character of biblical statements bearing upon the subject, they will be welcomed as a strong and highly satisfactory confirmation of the ancient, orthodox faith.

***Copies sent, postpaid, on receipt of price.

THOMAS WHITTAKER,

2 and 3 Bible House,   New York

www.ingramcontent.com/pod-product-compliance
Lightning Source LLC
Chambersburg PA
CBHW030304170426
43202CB00009B/862